Editor
Erica N. Russikoff, M.A.

Illustrator
Clint McKnight

Cover Artist
Brenda DiAntonis

Editor in Chief
Ina Massler Levin, M.A.

Creative Director
Karen J. Goldfluss, M.S. Ed.

Art Coordinator
Renée Christine Yates

Imaging
Craig Gunnell

Publisher
Mary D. Smith, M.S. Ed.

Differentiated Nonfiction Reading

GRADE 6

Includes Standards & Benchmarks

- Each passage is written at 3 different levels: easier, average, more challenging
- Content areas include Science, Geography, History, and Language Arts

Teacher Created Resources

Author

Debra J. Housel, M.S. Ed.

Teacher Created Resources, Inc.
6421 Industry Way
Westminster, CA 92683
www.teachercreated.com

ISBN: 978-1-4206-2923-1

© 2010 Teacher Created Resources, Inc.
Made in U.S.A.

Teacher Created Resources

Table of Contents

Introduction

If you are like most teachers, your classroom includes a wide variety of students: average students, English language learners, gifted students, and learning disabled students. You may be expected to get your diverse student population, including special education students and those for whom English is a second language, to master grade-level, content-area material. That's a challenging task and one that requires grade-level, content-area materials written at several levels. *Differentiated Nonfiction Reading* was written specifically to help you respond to the demands of your state and local standards while meeting the needs of your students.

Purpose of This Book

Each passage in *Differentiated Nonfiction Reading* covers a grade-level appropriate curriculum topic in science, geography, history, or language arts. The Mid-continent Research for Education and Learning (McREL) standard and benchmark related to each passage is listed on pages 9–12.

Each content-area passage is written at three different levels: easy (below grade level), average (at grade level), and challenging (above grade level). After each passage is a set of comprehension questions that all of your students will answer. This enables your students to access the text and concepts at their instructional—rather than frustration—level, while requiring them to meet objective standards, just as they must do on standardized assessments.

Prepare Your Students to Read Content-Area Text

You can prepare your students to read the passages in *Differentiated Nonfiction Reading* by daily reading aloud a short nonfiction selection from another source. Reading content-area text aloud is critical to developing your students' ability to read it themselves.

Discussing content-area concepts with your class is also very important. Remember, however, that discussion can never replace reading aloud since people do not speak using the vocabulary and complex sentence structures of written language.

Readability

All of the passages in *Differentiated Nonfiction Reading* have a reading level that has been calculated by the Flesch-Kincaid Readability Formula. This formula, built into Microsoft Word®, determines a text's readability by calculating the number of words, syllables, and sentences.

Each passage is presented at three levels: easy, average, and challenging. *Easy* is below sixth-grade level; *average* is at sixth-grade level; and *challenging* is above sixth-grade level. The chart on page 13 shows you the specific reading levels of every passage.

To ensure that only you know the reading level at which each student is working, the levels are not printed on the passages. Instead, at the top of the page is a set of books with a specific pattern that will allow you to quickly match students and passages.

Pattern			
Reading Level	**easy** (below grade level)	**average** (at grade level)	**challenging** (above grade level)

Introduction *(cont.)*

Essential Comprehension Skills

Comprehension is the primary goal of any reading task. Students who comprehend expository text not only do better on tests, but they also have more opportunities in life. *Differentiated Nonfiction Reading* will help you to promote the foundation of comprehension skills necessary for a lifetime of learning. The questions following each passage always appear in the same order and cover six vital comprehension skills:

1. **Locating facts**—Questions based on exactly what the text states—*who, what, when, where, why,* and *how many*

2. **Understanding vocabulary in context**—Questions based on the ability to infer word meaning from the syntax and semantics of the surrounding text, as well as the ability to recognize known synonyms and antonyms for a newly encountered word

3. **Determining sequence**—Questions based on chronological order—what happened *first, last,* and *in between*

4. **Identifying conditions**—Questions that ask students to identify similarities and differences or notice cause-and-effect relationships

5. **Making inferences**—Questions that require students to evaluate, make decisions, and draw logical conclusions

6. **Analyzing and visualizing**—Questions that make students draw upon their schema and/or visualization skills to select the correct response (Visualization reinforces the important skill of picturing the text.)

How to Use This Book

You can choose to do whole-class or independent practice. For whole-group practice, you can:

1. Distribute the passages based on students' instructional reading levels.

2. Have students read the text silently and answer the questions either on the comprehension questions page or on one of the Answer Sheets on pages 94–95.

3. Collect all of the papers and score them.

4. Return the comprehension questions pages or Answer Sheets to the students, and discuss how they determined their answers.

5. Point out how students had to use their background knowledge to answer certain questions.

You may distribute the passages without revealing the different levels. There are several ways to approach this. If you do not want your students to be aware that the passages are differentiated, organize the passages in small piles by seating arrangement. Then, when you approach a group of desks, you have just the levels you need. An alternative is to make a pile of passages from diamonds to polka dots. Put a finger between the top two levels. Then, as you approach each student, pull the passage from the top (easy), middle (average), or bottom (challenging) layer. You will need to do this quickly and without much hesitation.

Introduction *(cont.)*

How to Use This Book *(cont.)*

You can also announce to your class that all students will read at their own instructional levels. Do not discuss the technicalities of how the reading levels were determined. Just state that every person is reading at his or her own level and then answering the same questions. By making this statement, you can make distributing the three different levels a straightforward process.

If you find that a student is doing well, try giving him or her the next-level-up passage the next time. If he or she displays frustration, be ready to slip the student the lower-level passage.

If you prefer to have the students work independently or in centers, follow this procedure:

1. Create a folder for each student.
2. If needed, make photocopies of the Answer Sheet on page 95 for each class member, and staple the Answer Sheet to the back of each student folder.
3. Each time you want to use a passage, place the appropriate reading level of the passage and the associated comprehension questions in each student's folder.
4. Have students retrieve their folders, read the passage, and answer the questions.
5. Go over the answers with the whole class, or check the folders individually at a convenient time.
6. As an option, you may want to provide a laminated copy of the Answer Key on page 96 in the center, so students can check their own papers.

Teaching Multiple-Choice Response

Whichever method you choose for using this book, it's a good idea to practice as a class how to read a passage and respond to the comprehension questions. In this way, you can demonstrate your own thought processes by "thinking aloud" to figure out an answer. Essentially, this means that you tell your students your thoughts as they come to you.

First, make copies of the practice comprehension questions on page 8, and distribute them to your class. Then, make and display an overhead transparency of the practice reading passage on page 7. Next, read the passage chorally. Studies have found that students of all ages enjoy choral reading, and it is especially helpful for English language learners. Choral reading lets students practice reading fluently in a safe venue because they can read in a whisper or even drop out if they feel the need.

Discuss Question 1: After you've read the passage aloud, ask a student to read the first question aloud. Tell the student NOT to answer the question. Instead, read all of the answer choices aloud. Emphasize that reading the choices first is always the best way to approach any multiple-choice question. Since the question is about *locating facts*, reread the first paragraph of the passage aloud as the class follows along. Have the students reread the question silently and make a selection based on the information found. Ask a student who gives the correct response (C) to explain his or her reasoning. Explain that the first question is always the easiest because the fact is stated right in the passage.

Discuss Question 2: The second question is about the *vocabulary* word shown in boldfaced print in the passage. Ask a student to read the question aloud. Teach your students to reread the sentence before, the sentence with, and the sentence after the vocabulary word in the passage. This will give them a context and help them to figure out what the word means. Then, have them substitute the word choices given for the vocabulary term in the passage. For each choice, they should reread the sentence with the substituted word and ask themselves, "Does this make sense?" This will help them to identify the best choice. One by one, substitute the words into the sentence, and read the sentence aloud. It will be obvious which one makes the most sense (A).

Teacher Created Resources, Inc. 5 #2923 Differentiated Nonfiction Reading

Introduction *(cont.)*

Teaching Multiple-Choice Response *(cont.)*

Discuss Question 3: The third question asks about *sequence*. Ask a student to read the question aloud. Write the choices on chart paper or the board. As a class, determine their order of occurrence, and write the numbers one through four next to them. Then, reread the question and make the correct choice (B).

Discuss Question 4: The fourth question is about *cause and effect* or *similarities and differences*. Ask a student to read the question aloud. Teach your students to look for the key words in the question ("pump water down") and search for those specific words in the passage. Explain that they may need to look for synonyms for the key words. For this question, ask your students to show where they found the correct response in the passage. Have students explain in their own words how they figured out the correct answer (D). This may be time-consuming at first, but it is an excellent way to help your students learn from each other.

Discuss Question 5: The fifth question asks students to make an *inference*. Ask a student to read the question aloud. Tell your students your thoughts as they occur to you, such as: "Well, the article didn't say that it is free to generate geothermal power, so that one's questionable. The article did say that geothermal energy comes from Earth, not from the sun, air, and water. So I'll get rid of that choice. We do have a lot of water, and in most places, that's what is forced down into Earth to make the steam. But you need to have a place where Earth is really hot near its surface, so it's not just a matter of having a water supply. I don't think that's the best choice here. Let's look back at the passage . . . it does state that there's an endless amount of heat rising from Earth, and we know that fossil fuels will soon be used up. Something that's endless cannot be used up, so I'm going to select D."

Discuss Question 6: The sixth question calls for *analysis* or *visualization*. With such questions, some of the answers may be stated in the passage, but others may have different wording. Sometimes one or more of the answers must be visualized to ascertain the correct response.

After having a student read the question aloud, you can say, "This one is tricky. It's asking me to choose the one that *isn't* instead of the one that *is*. First, let's look at all of the choices. Then, we can ask ourselves which ones are problems with geothermal power. Only one of these is not an issue." Then, read the answer choices aloud and eliminate them one by one. Point out that the passage states that geothermal energy does not pollute groundwater, which is how you identify the correct answer (C).

Frequent Practice Is Ideal

The passages and comprehension questions in *Differentiated Nonfiction Reading* are time-efficient, allowing your students to practice these skills often. The more your students practice reading and responding to content-area comprehension questions, the more confident and competent they will become. Set aside time to allow your class to do every passage. If you do so, you'll be pleased with your students' improved comprehension of any nonfiction text, both within your classroom and beyond its walls.

Geothermal Power

Our Earth has a layer of hot rock below its crust in an area called the mantle. Where groundwater touches these hot rocks, it changes into steam. This steam enables people to make electricity without causing pollution. It's called geothermal power. *Geo* means Earth, and *thermal* means heat.

Italians built the first geothermal power station in 1904. They found a place where steam rose from the ground. They trapped the steam and sent it through pipes to turbines. Turbines are big and round and can spin very quickly. The steam made the turbines turn, which **generated** electrical power.

In most places, steam does not come up on its own. Instead, power stations pump water down to the mantle. Some of this water returns as steam to make turbines rotate and create electricity.

Geothermal energy is good for Earth and its wildlife. It does not damage the air, water, or soil. However, the steam can bring up minerals that harm the turbines. Also, workers must be careful around the steam, or they could get burned.

Someday all of the fossil fuels will be used up. Geothermal power can never get used up. That's why people hope to find more places and better ways to use geothermal power.

Geothermal Power

Directions: Darken the best answer choice.

1. "Geothermal" means _____ from Earth.
   - (A) steam
   - (B) energy
   - (C) heat
   - (D) water

2. The word **generated** means
   - (A) made.
   - (B) used.
   - (C) opened.
   - (D) wasted.

3. Of the following choices, which occurs last?
   - (A) Steam moves turbines.
   - (B) Electricity goes to homes.
   - (C) Steam is trapped in pipes.
   - (D) Electrical power is made.

4. Why would people pump water down to a layer of hot rock?
   - (A) to cool Earth's mantle
   - (B) to prevent steam from escaping
   - (C) to bring minerals to Earth's surface
   - (D) to create steam

5. Why can't geothermal power get used up as fossil fuels can?
   - (A) It costs nothing to generate geothermal power.
   - (B) Scientists know how to make geothermal energy from the sun, air, and water.
   - (C) We have a huge supply of water, which is what gives us geothermal power.
   - (D) There's an endless supply of heat coming from within Earth.

6. Which is *not* a problem related to geothermal power?
   - (A) Minerals can build up on the turbines.
   - (B) There are just a few places to tap the power.
   - (C) It causes salt to build up and damage the groundwater.
   - (D) The steam is dangerous if it comes in contact with workers.

Standards Correlation

Each passage and comprehension question in *Differentiated Nonfiction Reading* meets at least one of the following standards and benchmarks, which are used with permission from McREL. Copyright 2010 McREL. Mid-continent Research for Education and Learning, 4601 DTC Boulevard, Suite 500, Denver, CO 80237. Telephone: 303-337-0990. Web site: *www.mcrel.org/standards-benchmarks*

Standards and Benchmarks	Passage Title	Pages
SCIENCE		
Standard 3. Understands the composition and structure of the universe and Earth's place in it **Benchmark 6.** Knows that the universe consists of many billions of galaxies (each containing many billions of stars) and that incomprehensible distances (measured in light years) separate these galaxies and stars from one another and from Earth	Stargazers	14–17
Standard 4. Understands the principles of heredity and related concepts **Benchmark 5.** Knows that the characteristics of an organism can be described in terms of a combination of traits; some traits are inherited, and others result from interaction with its environment	Margaret Mead, Anthropologist	18–21
Standard 7. Understands biological evolution and the diversity of life **Benchmark 1.** Knows basic ideas related to biological evolution (e.g., diversity of species is developed through gradual processes over many generations; biological adaptations, such as changes in structure, behavior, or physiology, allow some species to enhance their reproductive success and survival in a particular environment)	Similar Evolution: Zebras and Guinea Pigs	22–25
Standard 12. Understands the nature of scientific inquiry **Benchmark 2.** Understands that questioning, response to criticism, and open communication are integral to the process of science	Secrets Hamper Science	26–29
Standard 13. Understands the scientific enterprise **Benchmark 1.** Knows that people of all backgrounds and with diverse interests, talents, qualities, and motivations engage in fields of science and engineering; some of these people work in teams and others work alone, but all communicate extensively with others	Margaret Mead, Anthropologist	18–21
Benchmark 2. Knows that the work of science requires a variety of human abilities, qualities, and habits of mind	Stargazers	14–17
Benchmark 3. Knows various settings in which scientists and engineers may work (e.g., colleges and universities, businesses and industries, research institutes, government agencies)	The U.S. Army Corps of Engineers	30–33

Standards Correlation (cont.)

Standards and Benchmarks	Passage Title	Pages
GEOGRAPHY		
Standard 9. Understands the nature, distribution and migration of human populations on Earth's surface **Benchmark 1.** Understands demographic concepts and how they are used to describe population characteristics of a country or region (e.g., rates of natural increase, crude birth and death rates, infant mortality, population growth rates, doubling time, life expectancy, average family size)	Is Earth Overpopulated?	50–53
Standard 11. Understands the patterns and networks of economic interdependence on Earth's surface **Benchmark 1.** Understands the spatial aspects of systems designed to deliver goods and services (e.g., the movement of a product from point of manufacture to point of use; imports, exports, trading patterns of various countries; interruptions in world trade such as war, crop failures, and labor strikes)	Economies Are Connected	34–37
Standard 14. Understands how human actions modify the physical environment **Benchmark 1.** Understands the environmental consequences of people changing the physical environment (e.g., the effects of ozone depletion, climate change, deforestation, land degradation, soil salinization and acidification, ocean pollution, groundwater-quality decline, using natural wetlands for recreational and housing development)	Saving Earth One Bag at a Time	38–41
Standard 15. Understands how physical systems affect human systems **Benchmark 6.** Knows the ways in which humans prepare for natural hazards (e.g., earthquake preparedness, constructing houses on stilts in flood-prone areas, designation of hurricane shelters and evacuation routes in hurricane-prone areas)	Humans Versus Natural Disasters	42–45
Standard 16. Understands the changes that occur in the meaning, use, distribution, and importance of resources **Benchmark 7.** Understands how the development and widespread use of alternative energy sources (e.g., solar, wind, thermal) might have an impact on societies (in terms of air and water quality, existing energy industries, and current manufacturing practices)	That's Not Just Sunshine—It's Energy!	46–49
Standard 18. Understands global development and environmental issues **Benchmark 2.** Understands the possible impact that present conditions and patterns of consumption, production, and population growth might have on the future spatial organization of Earth	Is Earth Overpopulated?	50–53

#2923 Differentiated Nonfiction Reading   10   ©Teacher Created Resources, Inc.

Standards Correlation *(cont.)*

Standards and Benchmarks	Passage Title	Pages
WORLD HISTORY		
Standard 28. Understands how large territorial empires dominated much of Eurasia between the 16th and 18th centuries **Benchmark 2.** Understands how China viewed its role in the world during the Ming Dynasty (e.g., why China's attitude toward external political and commercial relations changed after the Zheng He voyages from 1405 to 1433)	Ancient Chinese Inventions	54–57
Standard 8. Understands how Aegean civilization emerged and how interrelations developed among peoples of the Eastern Mediterranean and Southwest Asia from 600 to 200 BCE **Benchmark 2.** Understands the major cultural elements of Greek society (e.g., the major characteristics of Hellenic sculpture, architecture, and pottery and how they reflected or influenced social values and culture; characteristics of Classical Greek art and architecture and how they are reflected in modern art and architecture; Socrates' values and ideas as reflected in his trial; how Greek gods and goddesses represent nonhuman entities, and how gods, goddesses, and humans interact in Greek myths)	The Seven Wonders of the Ancient World	58–61
Standard 39. Understands the causes and global consequences of World War I **Benchmark 1.** Understands the origins and significant features of World War I (e.g., the precipitating causes of the war; the factors that led to military stalemate in some areas; which countries joined each of the two alliances—the Allied Powers and the Central Powers—and the advantages and disadvantages for the formation of alliances; major areas of combat in Europe and Southwest Asia) **Benchmark 2.** Understands the immediate and long-term consequences of World War I (e.g., the principal theaters of conflict in World War I in Europe, Southeast Asia, sub-Saharan Africa, East Asia, and the South Pacific; major turning points in the war; the short-term demographic, social, economic, and environmental consequences of the war's violence and destruction; the hardships of trench warfare)	Germany and World War I	62–65
U.S. HISTORY		
Standard 31. Understands economic, social, and cultural developments in the contemporary United States **Benchmark 4.** Understands aspects of contemporary American culture (e.g., the international influence of American culture, increased popularity of professional sports, influence of spectator sports on popular culture, sports, and entertainment figures who advertise specific products)	The Curse of the Bambino	66–69

Standards Correlation (cont.)

Standards and Benchmarks	Passage Title	Pages
U.S. HISTORY (cont.)		
Standard 31. (cont.) **Benchmark 5.** Understands contemporary issues concerning gender and ethnicity (e.g., the range of women's organizations, the changing goals of the women's movement, and the issues currently dividing women; issues involving justice and common welfare; how interest groups attempted to achieve their goals of equality and justice; how African, Asian, Hispanic, and Native Americans have shaped American life and retained their cultural heritage)	Barack Obama, 44th President of the United States	70–73
LANGUAGE ARTS*		
Standard 7. Uses reading skills and strategies to understand and interpret a variety of informational texts **Benchmark 1.** Uses reading skills and strategies to understand a variety of informational texts (e.g., electronic texts; textbooks; biographical sketches; directions; essays; primary source historical documents, including letters and diaries; print media, including editorials, news stories, periodicals, and magazines; consumer, workplace, and public documents, including catalogs, technical directions, procedures, and bus routes)	Robots (Encyclopedia Entry)	74–77
	Paul Newman (Web Page)	78–81
Benchmark 2. Knows the defining characteristics of a variety of informational texts (e.g., electronic texts; textbooks; biographical sketches; letters; diaries; directions; procedures; magazines; essays; primary source historical documents; editorials; news stories; periodicals; bus routes; catalogs; technical directions; consumer, workplace, and public documents)	Visit the Bizarre Winchester Mansion (Tour Book Page)	82–85
	Viz-a-Phone (Public Service Advertisement)	86–89
Benchmark 4. Uses new information to adjust and extend personal knowledge base		
Benchmark 5. Draws conclusions and makes inferences based on explicit and implicit information in texts **Benchmark 6.** Differentiates between fact and opinion in informational texts	Native American Unsolved Mysteries (Back of Book)	90–93

*Every passage in this book meets the language arts standard and some or all of these benchmarks. The language arts passages are listed here because they were designed to specifically address these benchmarks.

Reading Levels Chart

Content Area and Title	Easy ◇	Average ☆	Challenging ◯
SCIENCE			
Stargazers	4.6	6.1	7.3
Margaret Mead, Anthropologist	5.0	6.4	7.3
Similar Evolution: Zebras and Guinea Pigs	4.7	6.3	7.4
Secrets Hamper Science	4.3	6.5	7.9
The U.S. Army Corps of Engineers	5.3	6.4	7.9
GEOGRAPHY			
Economies Are Connected	4.8	6.2	7.5
Saving Earth One Bag at a Time	4.2	6.2	7.5
Humans Versus Natural Disasters	5.5	6.8	7.7
That's Not Just Sunshine—It's Energy!	4.9	6.0	7.6
Is Earth Overpopulated?	5.6	6.7	7.6
WORLD AND U.S. HISTORY			
Ancient Chinese Inventions	5.2	6.1	7.4
The Seven Wonders of the Ancient World	4.4	6.4	7.5
Germany and World War I	5.2	6.2	7.3
The Curse of the Bambino	5.0	6.3	7.3
Barack Obama, 44th President of the United States	5.7	6.8	7.8
LANGUAGE ARTS			
Robots (Encyclopedia Entry)	4.7	6.0	8.1
Paul Newman (Web Page)	4.0	6.1	8.0
Visit the Bizarre Winchester Mansion (Tour Book Page)	4.4	6.1	8.0
Viz-a-Phone (Public Service Advertisement)	5.5	6.7	7.9
Native American Unsolved Mysteries (Back of Book)	5.3	6.3	8.0

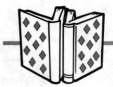

Stargazers

Science is a field that is always changing. Knowledge grows. How? New ideas build upon old. Things that scientists did decades ago form the basis for today's understandings. Two female astronomers helped to change what we know about stars and galaxies. One was Annie Jump Cannon. The other was Henrietta Swan Leavitt.

Annie Jump Cannon was born in 1863. The Civil War was raging. At that time, few women attended high school. Almost none went to college. Annie's mother loved to stargaze. She taught her daughter all that she knew about the stars. Annie liked to learn. She wanted to know more. Her teachers got her parents to send her to college. While she was there, she had an ear infection. It left her hearing impaired. There were no hearing aids back then. She had to learn to read lips.

Annie graduated. She went to work. She got a job in the Harvard College **Observatory**. She was hired because she was good at noticing details. Her job was hard. For 25 cents an hour, she studied glass photographic plates. The plates were full of stars. These star photos were taken by combining cameras and telescopes. The pictures showed the light each star made. Annie studied the pictures. She looked at the same ones each day. Were they getting brighter? Were they dimmer? Were they in the same spot? Then, Annie had to classify the stars. She found that the old classification method didn't work. So she came up with a new one. Her star classification system is still used today. Between 1915 and 1924, she wrote nine volumes of the *Henry Draper Catalog*. It is a book. Astrophysicists still use it today. Annie worked until she was seventy-seven years old. She catalogued more than 350,000 stars. She also found five novas. Novas are stars that suddenly become very bright and then fade. In 1931, she won an award. It was the Draper Medal from the National Academy of Sciences.

Annie was one of a team of women. They all worked to catalog the stars. Henrietta Swan Leavitt was another stargazer. She worked in the same place. She was deaf, too. Henrietta made the Harvard Standard scale in 1913. It was used to measure a star's brightness. Henrietta was interested in variable stars. These stars changed in brightness. Each one followed a cycle, like a schedule. She tracked each star over time. She found 2,400 variable stars. Today, we know that there are more than 24,000.

Henrietta figured out why the variable stars had cycles. It was based on how far away they were. She came up with the Period-Luminosity Law in 1908. This law lets scientists measure where stars lie beyond the Milky Way Galaxy. For the first time, people knew for sure that there were stars outside our own galaxy. Later, the astronomer Edwin Hubble used this law. He proved there are stars and whole galaxies beyond our own.

Henrietta died in 1921. Annie lived until 1941.

Stargazers

Science is a field that is always growing because new knowledge builds upon old. Things that scientists did decades ago form the basis for today's understandings. Two female astronomers helped to improve what we know about stars and galaxies. One was Annie Jump Cannon. The other was Henrietta Swan Leavitt.

When Annie Jump Cannon was born in 1863, the Civil War was raging. At that time, few women attended high school. Almost none went to college. Annie's mother loved to stargaze. She taught her daughter all that she knew about the stars. Annie was fascinated. She wanted to know more. Her teachers convinced her parents to send her to Wellesley College. While she was there, she had an ear infection. It left her hearing impaired. There were no hearing aids back then. She had to learn to read lips.

After she graduated, she went to work. She got a job in the Harvard College **Observatory**. She was hired because she was good at observing details. Her job was tough. For 25 cents an hour, she studied glass photographic plates full of stars. These star photos were taken by combining cameras with telescopes. The pictures showed the differing bands of light each star made. She looked at the same ones each day to determine if the stars were growing brighter or dimmer. She determined if they were staying in the same position, too. While studying the pictures, Annie had to classify the stars. She soon found that the old classification method didn't work. So she came up with the star classification system that is used today. Between 1915 and 1924, she wrote nine volumes of the *Henry Draper Catalog*. It is a book that astrophysicists still use today. Annie worked until she was seventy-seven years old. She catalogued more than 350,000 stars. She also discovered five novas. Novas are stars that suddenly become brighter and then fade. In 1931, she won the Draper Medal from the National Academy of Sciences.

Annie was one of a team of women who worked to catalog the stars. Henrietta Swan Leavitt was another stargazer in the same observatory. Like Annie, Henrietta was also deaf. Henrietta made the Harvard Standard scale in 1913. It was used to measure a star's brightness. Henrietta became interested in variable stars. These stars' brightness changed. They followed a cycle, like a schedule. She monitored each star over time. She found 2,400 variable stars. Today, we know that there are more than 24,000.

Henrietta figured out that the variable stars' cycles came from distance. She came up with the Period-Luminosity Law in 1908. Scientists use this to measure where stars lie beyond the Milky Way Galaxy. For the first time, people knew for sure that there were stars outside our own galaxy. Later, the famous astronomer Edwin Hubble used this law to prove that there are stars—and whole galaxies—beyond our own.

Henrietta died in 1921, while Annie lived until 1941.

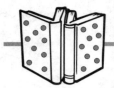

Stargazers

Science is a field that is always expanding. New knowledge builds upon old. Things that scientists did decades ago provide the basis for today's more advanced understandings. Two female astronomers helped to improve our knowledge of stars and galaxies. Their names were Annie Jump Cannon and Henrietta Swan Leavitt.

When Annie Jump Cannon was born in 1863, the Civil War was raging. At that time, few women attended high school, let alone college. Annie would break this mold. Her mother loved to stargaze, and she taught her all she knew about the stars. Annie was fascinated. She wanted to know more and got her teachers to convince her parents to send her to Wellesley College. While she was there, she had an ear infection that left her hearing impaired. There were no hearing aids back then, so she learned to read lips.

After she graduated, she started working in the Harvard College **Observatory**. She was hired because she was good at observing details. Her job was difficult. For 25 cents an hour, she studied glass photographic plates full of stars. These star photos were taken by combining cameras with telescopes equipped with prisms. The pictures showed the differing bands of light produced by each star. She looked at the same ones each day to answer three questions: Was each star in the same position? Was it any brighter than the day before? Was it dimmer? While studying the pictures, Annie had to classify the stars. She soon discovered that the old classification method didn't work. So she designed the star classification system that is used today. Between 1915 and 1924, she produced nine volumes of the *Henry Draper Catalog*, a guidebook that astrophysicists still use today. Annie worked until she was seventy-seven years old, cataloguing more than 350,000 stars and discovering five novas. Novas are stars that suddenly become much brighter and then fade. In 1931, she won the Draper Medal from the National Academy of Sciences.

Annie was one of a team of women working to catalog the stars. Henrietta Swan Leavitt was another deaf stargazer in the same observatory. She created the Harvard Standard scale in 1913. It was used to measure a star's brightness. Henrietta became interested in variable stars. These stars' brightness changed on a regular schedule. She tracked each star over time, discovering 2,400 variable stars. Today, we know of more than 24,000.

Henrietta figured out that the variable stars' cycles were related to distance. She came up with the Period-Luminosity Law in 1908. Scientists use this to measure where stars lie beyond the Milky Way Galaxy. For the first time, everyone knew for certain that there were stars outside our own galaxy. Later, the famous astronomer Edwin Hubble used this law to prove that there are not only stars but entire galaxies beyond our own.

Henrietta died in 1921, while Annie lived until 1941.

Stargazers

Directions: Darken the best answer choice.

1. Who proved that there are galaxies besides the Milky Way?
   - Ⓐ Annie Jump Cannon
   - Ⓑ Edwin Hubble
   - Ⓒ Henrietta Swan Leavitt
   - Ⓓ Henry Draper

2. An **observatory** is a place where
   - Ⓐ astronomers study the solar system.
   - Ⓑ college students earn degrees.
   - Ⓒ astronomers can travel to planets.
   - Ⓓ college students go to study for exams.

3. Which event occurred last?
   - Ⓐ Henrietta stated the Period-Luminosity Law.
   - Ⓑ Henrietta created the Harvard Standard scale.
   - Ⓒ Annie produced the first of a nine-volume star catalog.
   - Ⓓ Annie won the Draper Medal from the National Academy of Sciences.

4. Variable stars change
   - Ⓐ into novas.
   - Ⓑ in position.
   - Ⓒ in brightness.
   - Ⓓ in color.

5. What is the first name of the astronomer for whom the Hubble Telescope is named?
   - Ⓐ Annie
   - Ⓑ Edwin
   - Ⓒ Henry
   - Ⓓ Henrietta

6. Picture Annie and Henrietta at work in the Harvard College Observatory. What *don't* you see in their work area?
   - Ⓐ photographic plates
   - Ⓑ cameras
   - Ⓒ telescopes
   - Ⓓ computers

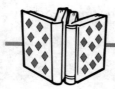

Margaret Mead, Anthropologist

Margaret Mead was a scientist. She discovered new things about the cultural and social lives of humans. She studied anthropology. It is a branch of science. It is the study of the beliefs and ways of life of different groups.

When she was born in 1901, her dad was a college professor. His job made him move around. By the time she was in middle school, Margaret had already lived in sixty places! This taught her to easily adapt to change. She found that she liked watching people. She longed to know what made families and other groups alike. She wanted to know: which behaviors were common to all?

Mead went to college. When she graduated, she went to Samoa. It is a group of islands. They are in the South Pacific. The nation lies between Hawaii and New Guinea. There she worked with sixty-eight teen girls. She wanted to see if hormones and physical changes caused teen problems. She thought that maybe the society caused too much pressure. She found that the girls in Samoa had an easier passage from childhood to womanhood than American girls did. She wrote about this in her first book.

Next, she went to New Guinea. There she lived with and studied three tribes. She wanted to see how the values of each culture affected the men and women. She was the first scientist to state that male and female traits often come from the culture. They aren't just caused by basic physical differences. In one tribe, both men and women were equal. They raised their children together. In another tribe, the men and women seemed heartless. Their children had to fend for themselves. It was clear that culture played a big role in rearing children.

Margaret Mead

Later, she went to Bali. She had young children draw pictures. Their drawings helped her to understand how they viewed their world. When Mead studied the children, she used scientific methods. She had certain ways of interviewing and observing people. She had methods of note-taking and photographing them, too. Her standards are still used by anthropologists today.

Mead helped people to understand that cultures differ in the actions they view as good and bad. What is seen as polite in one society might be rude in another. She had a keen awareness about cultures and the motivation of the people living within them. In World War II, her **expertise** helped the U.S. military when she explained the cultures of Germany and Japan.

She once said, "Never doubt that a small group of thoughtful, committed people can change the world. Indeed, it is the only thing that ever has." She lived those words. Besides anthropology, her work led to more knowledge in the fields of sociology and psychology. Mead died in 1978.

Margaret Mead, Anthropologist

Margaret Mead was a scientist who studied the cultural and social lives of humans. She was an anthropologist. In this branch of science, people study the beliefs and ways of life of different groups.

Her father was a college professor when she was born in 1901. Professor Mead's job required that he move around a lot. By the time she was in middle school, Margaret had already lived in sixty different places! This enabled her to easily adapt to different places. As she grew older, she found she liked watching people. She longed to know what made families and other groups different. She wondered: which behaviors were common to all?

Mead went to college. When she graduated, she went to Samoa. Samoa is a group of islands in the South Pacific. It lies halfway between Hawaii and New Guinea. There she worked with sixty-eight teen girls. She wanted to see if hormones and physical changes caused teen problems. She thought that perhaps the problems came from society's pressures. She found that the girls in Samoa had an easier transition from childhood to womanhood than American girls did. She wrote about this in her first book.

Next, she went to New Guinea. There she lived with and studied three different tribes. She wanted to see how the values of different cultures affected the roles of men and women. She was the first scientist to state that male and female traits often come from the culture rather than basic physical differences. In one tribe, both men and women were equal and raised their children together. In another tribe, the men and women seemed heartless and made their children fend for themselves. From this, she concluded that culture played a big role in rearing children.

Margaret Mead

Later, she went to Bali to focus on young children. She had them draw pictures. Their drawings helped her to understand how the children viewed their world. When Mead studied these children, she developed scientific methods. She had certain ways of interviewing, observing, note-taking, and photographing human subjects. Her standards are still used by anthropologists today.

Mead helped people to understand that cultures differ in the behaviors they consider good and bad. What is considered polite in one society might be rude in another. She had keen skills of observation about cultures and the motivation of the people living within them. Her **expertise** helped the U.S. military. During World War II, she analyzed the cultures of Germany and Japan.

She once said, "Never doubt that a small group of thoughtful, committed people can change the world. Indeed, it is the only thing that ever has." She lived those words. Besides anthropology, her work led to advancements in the fields of sociology and psychology. When Mead died in 1978, the world lost a trailblazer.

Margaret Mead, Anthropologist

Margaret Mead was an anthropologist who studied the cultural and social lives of humans, and she discovered new things. Anthropology is the study of the beliefs and ways of life of different groups.

Her father was a college professor when she was born in 1901. Professor Mead's job required that he move around a lot. By the time she was in middle school, Margaret had already lived in sixty different places! This enabled her to easily adapt to different places. As she grew older, she found she liked watching people. She longed to know the similarities shared by families and other groups.

Mead attended college. When she graduated, she went to Samoa, a group of islands in the South Pacific that lies halfway between Hawaii and New Guinea. There she worked with sixty-eight teen girls. She wanted to see if hormones and physical changes caused teen problems. She thought that the problems came from society's pressures. She found that the girls in Samoa had an easier transition from childhood to womanhood than American girls did. She wrote about her findings in her first book.

Next, she went to New Guinea. There she lived with three different tribes. She wanted to see how the values of different cultures affected the roles of men and women. She was the first scientist to state that male and female traits often come from the culture rather than basic physical differences. In one tribe, both men and women were equal and raised their children together. In another tribe, the men and women seemed heartless and made their children fend for themselves. These observations led Mead to believe that culture played a major role in rearing children.

Later, she went to Bali to focus on young children. She asked them to draw pictures. Their drawings helped her to understand how the children viewed their world. When Mead studied these children, she developed scientific methods. She had certain ways of interviewing, observing, note-taking, and photographing human subjects. Her standards are still used by anthropologists today.

Margaret Mead

Mead helped people to understand that cultures differ in the behaviors they promote and discourage. What is considered polite in one society might be rude in another. She had keen skills of observation about cultures and the motivation of the people living within them. Her **expertise** helped the U.S. military to understand the cultures of Germany and Japan during World War II.

She once said, "Never doubt that a small group of thoughtful, committed people can change the world. Indeed, it is the only thing that ever has." She lived those words. In addition to anthropology, her work led to advancements in the fields of sociology and psychology. When Mead died in 1978, the world lost a trailblazer.

Margaret Mead, Anthropologist

Directions: Darken the best answer choice.

1. What *didn't* Mead do?
   - Ⓐ teach college psychology and sociology
   - Ⓑ write multiple books
   - Ⓒ develop scientific methods for anthropology
   - Ⓓ form theories about what motivates human behavior

2. The word **expertise** means
   - Ⓐ intelligence.
   - Ⓑ expert knowledge.
   - Ⓒ money.
   - Ⓓ job.

3. Which event happened third?
   - Ⓐ Mead studied teenagers in Samoa.
   - Ⓑ Mead moved to sixty different places.
   - Ⓒ Mead studied gender roles in New Guinea.
   - Ⓓ Mead studied little children in Bali.

4. An *anthropologist* is a person who studies
   - Ⓐ New Guinea, Samoa, and Bali.
   - Ⓑ children and teenagers.
   - Ⓒ Japan and Germany.
   - Ⓓ human culture.

5. You can tell that Mead enjoyed
   - Ⓐ observing and learning about different societies.
   - Ⓑ teaching people how to be polite.
   - Ⓒ living in sixty different homes as a child.
   - Ⓓ studying male behavior more than female behavior.

6. A society teaches that men are hunters and women are homemakers. In this society, you would expect to see
   - Ⓐ males gathering fruits and nuts and females hunting.
   - Ⓑ males getting food and females cooking it.
   - Ⓒ males raising crops and females making clothes.
   - Ⓓ males and females sharing equally in childcare.

Similar Evolution:
Zebras and Guinea Pigs

Most people can instantly recognize zebras and guinea pigs. These animals do not look alike. One has long legs; the other has short legs. One has a tail; the other does not. They developed on different continents, too. Yet they are more alike than you may know. It's due to their separate evolution in nearly identical environments.

Evolution is based on survival of the fittest. The animals in a species that adapt the best to the conditions in which they live will survive. They will have a chance to reproduce. When two species face **comparable** stresses in their physical surroundings, the successful members of both tend to have the same survival features. Zebras and guinea pigs both originated in flat, grassy places. Zebras reside in Africa. Guinea pigs are native to South America. Both are prey animals. This means that they developed ways to avoid predators. So what behaviors and physical features do they share?

Zebras and guinea pigs are herd animals. They feel safest in a group. Each member of the group uses its senses to detect danger. Both species have eyes located on the sides of their heads. It gives them a wide field of vision. This helps them keep watch for predators. When a predator approaches, members use warning sounds and evasive actions. This alerts the whole group. The young of both species are born with full coats of hair and open eyes. Within hours of birth, both babies can run and eat solid food as well as their mothers' milk. Why? The ability to move with the herd offers protection. The young are kept close to the center of the herd.

The food that both species eat is coarse grass and shrubs. It wears down the teeth of these herbivores. To make up for this, the teeth of zebras and guinea pigs grow all of the time. And both have incisors for tearing plants and molars for grinding them. Since their food sources are almost the same, so are their digestive tracts.

Of course, the two species have differences, too. For example, a zebra can outrun a predator. If need be, it can stomp on, kick, or bite its enemy, too. A guinea pig can only try to outrun, outmaneuver, or hide. Wild guinea pigs have a very short life span compared to zebras. To make up for this problem, a guinea pig can get pregnant at four weeks of age and have litters of three to seven pups every ten weeks. A female zebra, on the other hand, cannot have babies so young. She must be at least three years old. She will give birth to just one foal a year. Wild guinea pigs (not the ones you see in the pet store) are mostly brown. Their camouflage coloring helps them to blend in with the ground. Zebras have stripes to confuse predators. When they run from a lion or a leopard, their coats look like waving grasses. This makes it harder for a big cat to pick out a single zebra from the running herd.

Similar Evolution: Zebras and Guinea Pigs

Zebras and guinea pigs are two animals that most people instantly recognize. They certainly don't look alike. One has long legs; the other has short legs. One has a tail; the other does not. They have homes on different continents, too. Yet they are more alike than you may realize. It's due to their separate evolution in nearly identical environments.

Evolution is based on survival of the fittest in a species. The animals that adapt the best to the conditions in which they live are the ones most apt to survive and reproduce. When two species experience **comparable** stresses in their physical surroundings, the successful members of both often have similar survival features. Zebras and guinea pigs both originated in flat, grassy regions. Zebras reside in Africa. Guinea pigs are native to South America. Both are prey animals, which means that they have developed methods to escape predators. So what behaviors and physical features are shared by both species?

Zebras and guinea pigs are herd animals. They are most comfortable when they are in a group. Each member of the group uses its senses to detect danger. Both species have eyes located on the sides of their heads to give them a wide field of vision. This helps them keep watch for predators. Members use warning sounds and evasive actions that alert the whole group when a predator approaches. The young of both species are born with full coats of hair and open eyes. In fact, within hours of birth, both babies can run and eat solid food in addition to their mothers' milk. Why? The ability to move with the herd provides protection. The young are usually kept close to the center of the herd.

The food that both species consume is coarse grass and shrubs. It wears down the teeth of these herbivores. To compensate for this, the teeth of zebras and guinea pigs grow continuously, and both have incisors for tearing vegetation and molars for grinding it. Since their food sources are nearly identical, so are their digestive tracts.

Of course, the two species have obvious differences, too. For example, a zebra can outrun a predator, or if need be, stomp on, kick, or bite its enemy. A guinea pig can only attempt to outrun, outmaneuver, or hide. Wild guinea pigs have a very short life span compared to zebras. To make up for this problem, a guinea pig can become pregnant at four weeks of age and produce litters of three to seven pups every ten weeks. A female zebra, on the other hand, cannot conceive until she is at least three years old. She will only give birth to one foal a year. Wild guinea pigs (not the ones you see in the pet store) are mostly brown. This camouflage coloring helps them to blend in with the ground. Zebras have stripes to confuse predators. When they run, their coats look like waving grasses to lions or leopards. This makes it harder for the predator to isolate a single zebra from the herd as it races across the grassy plain.

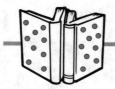

Similar Evolution:
Zebras and Guinea Pigs

Zebras and guinea pigs are two animals that most people instantly recognize, although they certainly don't look alike. One has long legs; the other has short legs. One has a tail; the other does not. They have homes on different continents, too. Yet, they are more alike than you may realize. It's due to their evolution in nearly identical environments.

Evolution is based on survival of the fittest in a species. The animals that adapt the best to the conditions in which they live are the ones most apt to survive and reproduce. When two species experience **comparable** environmental stresses, the successful members of both often possess similar survival traits. Zebras reside in Africa. Guinea pigs are native to South America. Yet zebras and guinea pigs both originated in flat, grassy regions. Both are prey animals and had to develop methods for evading predators. So what behaviors and physical features do both species share?

Zebras and guinea pigs are herd animals and feel safest within a group. Each member of the group uses its senses to detect danger and uses warning sounds and evasive actions to alert the whole group if a predator approaches. Both species have eyes located on the sides of their heads to give them a wide field of vision and enable them to efficiently spot predators. The young of both species are born with full coats of hair and open eyes. In fact, within hours of birth, both babies can run and eat solid food as well as their mothers' milk. The ability to move with the herd provides protection, and the young are usually kept close to the group's center.

Both species consume coarse grass and shrubs, which wear down these herbivores' teeth. To compensate, the teeth of zebras and guinea pigs grow continuously. Both have incisors for tearing vegetation and molars for grinding it. Since their food sources are nearly identical, so are their digestive tracts.

Of course, the two species have obvious differences, too. For example, a zebra can outrun, stomp on, kick, or bite its enemy, while a guinea pig can only attempt to outrun, outmaneuver, or hide. Compared to zebras, wild guinea pigs have a short life span. To make up for this problem, a guinea pig can become pregnant at four weeks of age and produce litters of three to seven pups every ten weeks. On the other hand, a female zebra cannot conceive until she is at least three years old, and then she will give birth to one foal each year. Wild guinea pigs (not the ones you see in the pet store) are brown; this coloring helps them to blend in with the ground. Zebras have stripes to confuse predators. When they run from lions and leopards, zebras' coats look like waving grasses. This makes it challenging for the predator to isolate a single animal from the herd whenever zebras gallop across the savannah.

Similar Evolution:
Zebras and Guinea Pigs

Directions: Darken the best answer choice.

1. Guinea pigs first originated in
   Ⓐ Africa.
   Ⓑ North America.
   Ⓒ South America.
   Ⓓ Central America.

2. The word **comparable** means
   Ⓐ similar.
   Ⓑ dissimilar.
   Ⓒ natural.
   Ⓓ intense.

3. Which event happens last?
   Ⓐ A female guinea pig can give birth to her first litter.
   Ⓑ A female guinea pig is kept near the group's center.
   Ⓒ A female zebra is kept in the center of the herd.
   Ⓓ A female zebra can give birth to her first foal.

4. What is the purpose of keeping zebra foals in the center of the herd?
   Ⓐ The foals can eat and run within hours of birth, so they can move with the herd.
   Ⓑ The foals cannot detect danger at the edges of the group.
   Ⓒ The adults hope to fend off a predator that tries to reach the foals.
   Ⓓ If a predator attacks, the adults can run in all directions, saving themselves, and leaving the foals behind.

5. Why do guinea pigs mate younger and have more babies each time than zebras?
   Ⓐ Guinea pigs have a steadier food supply than zebras.
   Ⓑ Guinea pigs have a shorter life span than zebras.
   Ⓒ Zebras can detect predators from farther away than guinea pigs.
   Ⓓ Guinea pigs live in larger herds than zebras do.

6. Think about an herbivore's teeth. You can tell that an herbivore is always
   Ⓐ an animal eaten as prey.
   Ⓑ a predator.
   Ⓒ independent.
   Ⓓ born able to eat solid foods immediately.

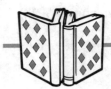

Secrets Hamper Science

During history, there have been times when knowledge did not get passed on. This means that advances were delayed because people did not share their discoveries with others. At times, science was held back for hundreds of years. In some cases, people wanted to keep a secret. In others, people just did not think to share.

Scurvy could cause death. It began with aches in the joints. Often, the victim's teeth fell out. Sufferers had purple blotches on their skin. They went crazy. At last, they could no longer eat. A lack of vitamin C caused scurvy. But no one knew that. It scared sailors. They were the most frequent victims. In 1536, Jacques Cartier, a French explorer, and his crew faced scurvy. They spent the winter months on the shore of the St. Lawrence River. More than two dozen men had died of scurvy. All the rest were dying. Then, a Native American found them. His name was Domagaya. He used tree bark to brew tea. The tree bark had vitamin C. Every man who drank the tea got better. But Cartier and his men did not bring back the tree bark. They did not tell anyone in Europe about the cure! Another 200 years passed. Many more people died. Then, scientists in Europe found that eating fresh fruits and vegetables cured scurvy. In 1795, the British navy said that all its sailors must eat limes. This ended scurvy in the British navy. Vitamin C was not understood until 1912.

Anton van Leeuwenhoek did not invent the microscope. Yet all of his life he kept improving microscopes. His were much better than the ones before. No one else had an instrument as good. He saw protozoa and bacteria under his scope. (He called both animalcules.) He shared his findings with the British Royal Society. But he kept the knowledge of how to make his lenses a secret. He died in 1723. He was ninety. His knowledge died with him. No one was able to duplicate his microscope for one hundred years. During that time, not much was learned about cells, bacteria, or algae.

Early American colonists built cobblestone homes. They made the walls of these houses with mortar and small stones. Their mortar was superior to any we have today. It stands up to weathering better. But no one wrote down how to make it. The ingredients are known. But there must be something else to the formula that has **eluded** scientists. It may be the temperature when mixed, amount of water added, length of drying time, or something else.

When information is not shared, the rate of invention slows down. Today, science and technology are making leaps and bounds. Why? Lots of information is available. Information is in journals, videos, podcasts, and on the Web. Facts given in a college lecture can be heard by people who were not there to hear the actual speech. Then, they can build on those ideas. The more people who have access to knowledge, the more minds are sparked by the information.

Secrets Hamper Science

Throughout history, there have been times when scientific knowledge was not passed on. This means that advances were delayed—sometimes for hundreds of years—because people failed to share their discoveries with others. In some cases, people wanted to keep a secret. In others, they just didn't think to share.

Scurvy was a deadly disease. It began with aches in the joints. Often, the victim's teeth fell out. Sufferers had purple blotches on their skin, then went crazy, and eventually lost the ability to eat. It was caused by a lack of vitamin C, but no one knew that. It terrorized sailors, who were the disease's most frequent victims. In 1536, Jacques Cartier, a French explorer, and his crew spent the winter months on the shore of the St. Lawrence River. More than two dozen men had died of scurvy, and all the rest were dying. Then, a Native American named Domagaya found them. He used tree bark to brew tea. The tree bark had lots of vitamin C. Every man who drank the tea recovered. But Cartier and his men never brought back the tree bark or shared this cure with anyone in Europe! It took 200 more years and countless deaths before anyone in Europe realized that eating fresh fruits and vegetables cured scurvy. In 1795, the British navy made limes a required food for all sailors. Scurvy vanished from the British navy. Vitamin C was not discovered until 1912.

Anton van Leeuwenhoek did not invent the first microscope. However, all of his life he kept improving microscopes. His were much better than any of the ones before. No one else had an instrument as good as his. He used his microscopes to discover protozoa and bacteria. (He called both animalcules.) He shared all of his findings with the British Royal Society. However, he kept the knowledge of how to make his lenses a secret. When he died in 1723 at the age of ninety, this knowledge died with him. No one was able to duplicate his microscope for a century. During that time, few new discoveries were made about cells, bacteria, or algae.

Hundreds of years ago, early American colonists built cobblestone homes. They made the walls of these houses with stones and mortar. They used a mortar that is superior to any we have today. It resists weathering better than today's mortar. But no one wrote down how to make it. The ingredients are known, but there must be something else to the formula—such as the temperature when mixed, amount of water added, or length of drying time—that has **eluded** current scientists.

When information is not shared, the rate of invention slows down. One of the reasons that science and technology are making such leaps and bounds today is that information is so readily available in journals, videos, podcasts, and on the Web. Information given at a lecture at a college can be accessed by people who were not in the audience. Then, they can build on those ideas. The more people who have access to knowledge, the more minds are stimulated by the information.

Secrets Hamper Science

Throughout history, there have been times when scientific knowledge was not passed on. This means that advances were delayed—sometimes for hundreds of years—because people failed to share their discoveries with others. In some cases, people wanted to keep a secret; in others, they just didn't think to share.

Scurvy was a deadly disease that began with aches in the joints. Often, the victim's teeth fell out. Sufferers had purple blotches on their skin, then went crazy, and eventually lost the ability to eat. It was caused by a lack of vitamin C, but no one knew that. Scurvy terrorized sailors, the disease's most frequent victims. In 1536, Jacques Cartier, a French explorer, and his crew spent the winter months on the shore of the St. Lawrence River. More than two dozen men had died of scurvy, and all the rest were dying of it. Then, a Native American named Domagaya found them and used a tree bark rich in vitamin C to brew a healing tea. Every man who drank the tea made a complete recovery. Yet Cartier and his men never brought back the tree bark or shared this cure with anyone in Europe! It took 200 more years and countless deaths before anyone in Europe realized that eating fresh fruits and vegetables cured scurvy. When the British navy made limes a required food for sailors in 1795, scurvy vanished from the British navy. Vitamin C was not discovered until 1912.

Anton van Leeuwenhoek did not invent the first microscope. However, all of his life he kept improving microscopes, and his were much better than any of the ones before. No one else in the world had instruments as good as his. He used his microscopes to discover protozoa and bacteria—although he called both animalcules. He shared all of his findings with the British Royal Society. However, he kept the knowledge of how to make his lenses a secret. Thus, when he died in 1723 at the age of ninety, this knowledge died with him. No one was able to duplicate his microscope for an entire century. During that time, little progress was made in the understanding of cells, bacteria, or algae.

Hundreds of years ago, early American colonists built cobblestone homes with walls of mortar and small stones. They used a mortar that is superior to any that we have today because it resists weathering better. Unfortunately, no one wrote down how to make it. Although the ingredients are known, there must be something else to the formula—such as the temperature when mixed, amount of water added, or length of drying time—that has **eluded** scientists.

When information is not shared, the rate of invention slows down. One of the reasons that science and technology are making such leaps and bounds today is that information is so readily available in journals, videos, podcasts, and on the Web. Information given at a lecture at a college can be accessed by people who were not there to hear the actual speech. Then, they can build on those ideas. The more people who have access to knowledge, the more minds are stimulated by the information.

Secrets Hamper Science

Directions: Darken the best answer choice.

1. Who invented the first microscope?
   - Ⓐ Anton van Leeuwenhoek
   - Ⓑ Jacques Cartier
   - Ⓒ Domagaya
   - Ⓓ The passage does not tell.

2. The word **eluded** means
   - Ⓐ informed.
   - Ⓑ overwhelmed.
   - Ⓒ escaped.
   - Ⓓ confused.

3. What happened first?
   - Ⓐ The British navy ended scurvy in its sailors.
   - Ⓑ Native Americans discovered the cure for scurvy.
   - Ⓒ Vitamin C was discovered.
   - Ⓓ Jacques Cartier and his men had scurvy.

4. *Mortar* is to *cobblestone wall* as
   - Ⓐ *thread* is to *pants*.
   - Ⓑ *book* is to *bookshelf*.
   - Ⓒ *tape* is to *tear*.
   - Ⓓ *sand* is to *castle*.

5. Why were sailors so often scurvy victims?
   - Ⓐ They ate too much salted fish at sea.
   - Ⓑ The salt in the sea air made their lungs susceptible to disease.
   - Ⓒ They refused to eat limes.
   - Ⓓ They did not have ready access to fresh fruits and vegetables at sea.

6. Anton van Leeuwenhoek's name for bacteria was probably a combination of the words
   - Ⓐ *Hercules* and *animal*.
   - Ⓑ *miniscule* and *animal*.
   - Ⓒ *ridicule* and *animal*.
   - Ⓓ *clue* and *animal*.

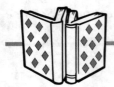
The U.S. Army Corps of Engineers

The U.S. Army Corps of Engineers is a branch of the U.S. Army. During a war, Corps members build bridges, roads, airfields, and camps for the military. The Corps' combat engineers find or build ways for troops to cross rivers. They plant and remove land and water mines. They may blow up roads and bridges. This is done to stop enemy troops from moving around. Combat engineers often come under enemy fire. They fight as ground troops.

The Corps began in 1802 when Congress set up West Point Military Academy. It was meant to train engineers. The U.S. Army Corps of Engineers constructed the Washington Monument in Washington, D.C. It helped to build the Chesapeake and Ohio Canal and the Panama Canal. Few people know that the Corps also managed the Manhattan Project during World War II. This project made the first atomic bomb.

During times of peace, the Corps plans and directs water resources. It keeps rivers navigable. It builds flood control structures. Some projects stop beach erosion and dredge harbors. Others build or repair dams and levees. The Corps manages and restores wetlands, too. It considers how a new project will impact the plants and animals that live in the area. By law, it must plan projects in such a way as to minimize damage. This means that the Corps does a study before starting any new project.

When there is a natural disaster, the Corps must take fast action to control the damage. One example is after the Mount St. Helens volcano erupted in 1980. It caused an avalanche of mud and debris that clogged rivers and streams. The Corps had to act quickly to prevent a worse disaster. It had to cut the risk of floods in populated areas downstream. It had to restore the rivers so that boats could safely navigate through them. It had to help a large area recover from the mudflow. Within days of the eruption, Corps members started working twenty-four hours a day. They dredged the rivers. This removed the excess **sediment**. The extra sediment put great pressure on levees. The Corps rushed to the levees. It built them up so that they would not burst.

A lot of debris from the volcano ended up in Spirit Lake. The lake's level rose 200 feet! A debris dam of dead trees blocked the lake's outlet to the river. Sooner or later, the water would burst through this blockage. That would cause a flash flood. The Corps had to drill a tunnel nearly two miles long. It drained some of that water into another creek. This prevented another disaster.

The U.S. Army Corps of Engineers

The U.S. Army Corps of Engineers is a branch of the U.S. Army. During a war, Corps members build bridges, roads, airfields, and camps for the military. The Corps' combat engineers find or build ways to help troops cross rivers. They plant and remove land and water mines. They may wreck roads and bridges to prevent enemy troops from reaching their destination. As a result, enemy fire gets aimed at combat engineers. They know how to fight as ground troops.

The Corps was organized in 1802. That's when Congress set up West Point Military Academy to train a group of engineers. The U.S. Army Corps of Engineers constructed the Washington Monument in Washington, D.C. It helped to build the Chesapeake and Ohio Canal and the Panama Canal. Few people know that the Corps also supervised the Manhattan Project. This World War II project built the first atomic bomb.

During times of peace, the Corps plans and directs water resources for the federal government. It keeps rivers navigable and builds flood control structures. Such projects include stopping beach erosion, dredging harbors, and repairing dams and levees. The Corps manages and restores wetlands, too. It considers the impact that a new project will have on the environment. By law, the Corps does a study before beginning any project. The idea is to reduce harm to the plants and animals that live in the area.

When there is a natural disaster, the Corps must take action. It tries to control the damage. For example, the Mount St. Helens volcano eruption in 1980 caused an avalanche. Mud and debris clogged waterways. The Corps had to act quickly. It had to cut the risk of floods in populated areas downstream and restore the rivers so that boats could safely navigate through them. It also had to help the area recover from the mudflow. Within days of the eruption, Corps members started working. They worked around the clock to dredge rivers to remove the excess **sediment**. The extra sediment put too much pressure on levees. The Corps rushed to the levees. It built them up so that they would not burst.

So much debris from the volcano ended up in Spirit Lake that the lake's level rose 200 feet! A debris dam of dead trees also blocked the lake's outlet to the river. At some point, the water would burst through this blockage. There would be a big flash flood. The Corps had to drill a tunnel nearly two miles long to drain some of that water away to another creek. This prevented another disaster.

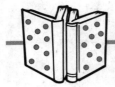

The U.S. Army Corps of Engineers

The U.S. Army Corps of Engineers is a branch of the U.S. Army. During a war, Corps members build bridges, roads, airfields, and camps for the military. The Corps' combat engineers find or build ways to help troops cross rivers. They plant and remove land and water mines. They may destroy roads and bridges to prevent enemy troops from reaching their destination. As a result, combat engineers often experience enemy fire. They know how to fight as ground troops.

The Corps was organized in 1802 when Congress set up West Point Military Academy to train a group of engineers. The U.S. Army Corps of Engineers constructed the Washington Monument in Washington, D.C., and helped to build the Chesapeake and Ohio Canal and the Panama Canal. Few people know that the Corps also supervised the Manhattan Project during World War II. This project developed the first atomic bomb.

During times of peace, the Corps plans and directs water resources and development for the federal government. It keeps rivers navigable and builds flood control structures. Its projects include stopping beach erosion, dredging harbors, and repairing dams and levees. The Corps manages and restores wetlands, too. It considers the impact that a new project will have on the plants and animals in the area. By law, it must plan projects to minimize damage. This means that the Corps does a study before undertaking any new project.

When there is a natural disaster, the Corps must take immediate action to control the damage. For example, after the Mount St. Helens volcano erupted in 1980, it caused an avalanche of mud and debris that blocked waterways. The Corps had to act quickly to prevent a worse disaster. It had to cut the risk of floods in populated areas downstream, restore the rivers so that boats could safely navigate through them, and help the area recover from the mudflow. Within days of the eruption, Corps members started working twenty-four hours a day. They dredged the rivers to remove the excess **sediment**. The extra sediment put enormous pressure on levees. The Corps rushed to the levees and built them up so that they would not burst.

So much debris from the volcano ended up in Spirit Lake that the lake's level rose 200 feet! A debris dam of dead trees also blocked the lake's outlet to the river. Eventually, the water would burst through this blockage and cause a flash flood. The Corps had to drill a tunnel nearly two miles long to carry some of that water away to another creek. This prevented another disaster.

The U.S. Army Corps of Engineers

Directions: Darken the best answer choice.

1. Which of these is *not* something that the U.S. Army Corps of Engineers would do?
   - Ⓐ repair dams
   - Ⓑ restore wetlands
   - Ⓒ fight wildfires
   - Ⓓ dredge rivers

2. The word **sediment** means
   - Ⓐ a levee built of sandbags.
   - Ⓑ a mudslide.
   - Ⓒ a debris dam.
   - Ⓓ solids that settle to the bottom of a liquid.

3. What happened last in the history of the U.S. Army Corps of Engineers?
   - Ⓐ The Corps drained extra water from Spirit Lake.
   - Ⓑ The Corps built the Washington Monument.
   - Ⓒ The Corps dredged waterways near Mount St. Helens.
   - Ⓓ The Corps supervised the Manhattan Project.

4. The Corps wants to build a new dam for hydroelectric power. What is the first step it must take?
   - Ⓐ determine the dimensions of the dam needed to generate a certain amount of power
   - Ⓑ do an environmental study to find the best location for the dam
   - Ⓒ hire contractors and workers to construct the dam
   - Ⓓ figure out what materials are needed to build the dam

5. The Missouri River is nearing flood stage. What might members of the U.S. Army Corps of Engineers be doing?
   - Ⓐ building a temporary bridge over the river
   - Ⓑ directing traffic near the river
   - Ⓒ managing water flow at dams to control the river level
   - Ⓓ removing animals from nearby wetlands

6. In which situation might you see the U.S. Army Corps of Engineers at work?
   - Ⓐ studying the effects of a proposed dam on a swamp
   - Ⓑ constructing the foundation of a skyscraper
   - Ⓒ operating a sewage treatment plant
   - Ⓓ building a pedestrian walkway over an expressway

Economies Are Connected

People have always traded with each other. Before money was invented, they bartered. It was not an efficient method. What if you wanted something that someone else had, but you didn't have anything they wanted? Then, there was no way to make the trade.

Now, money is used for trade. World banks keep track of how much one kind of money is worth compared to another on a daily basis. It is called an exchange rate. People in Japan can use yen to buy something in Mexican pesos. They just have to change their money based on the exchange rate on that day. It is easiest to buy foreign goods with a credit card. Then, the exchange rate gets figured out automatically. In Europe, many nations use the same currency. It is the euro. This makes buying and selling easy.

When goods leave one country to be sold in another, they are exported. Goods that are brought into one nation from another are imported. For example, in the United States, an imported car may come from Korea. A domestic car would be built in the United States. The United States imports a lot of oil and exports a lot of grain. The farms in the Midwest help to feed the world. The corn, oats, and wheat move through a network of railroads, highways, and shipping lanes.

The grain from the Midwest that will be exported must travel by train. It moves in a hopper car. The train goes to a shipping dock on a river or ocean. When it arrives, the hopper car is emptied. It is poured into the hold of a huge cargo ship. It takes many hopper cars to fill one cargo hold. Then, the ship moves across the sea. The grain is unloaded in another port. Next, it travels by train or truck to a company. That business grinds it and then makes it into bread, cereal, or other foods. Then, it travels by truck to a store.

Teak is a type of wood. It grows in the rain forests of Indonesia. Furniture is made from teak because it is a pretty color and resists rot. First, the teak trees must be chopped down. Then, the logs must be cut into lumber that's easy to transport. The lumber travels to an ocean-going vessel. When it arrives in the United States, the teak is unloaded. It is put onto train cars. The train carries it to a furniture manufacturer. The business makes teak boards into tables, chairs, and desks. Trucks move the finished furniture to a store.

If a nation imports more goods than it exports, there is a trade imbalance. This can cause economic problems. And because the world's economies are **interdependent**, a problem in one economy may cause trouble in others. Americans have money invested in foreign corporations. Foreigners have money invested in U.S. companies. Economies are linked together so that the fate of one affects them all. If one economy went into a deep slump called a depression, it could have a domino effect on the other major economies. As a result, they might all end up in a depressed state.

Economies Are Connected

From the dawn of time, people have traded with each other. Before money was invented, people bartered. It was an inefficient system. What if you wanted something that someone else had, but you didn't have anything they wanted? Then, there was no way to make the trade.

Now, money is used for trade. World banks keep track of how much one currency is worth compared to another on a daily basis. It is called an exchange rate. People in Japan can use yen to buy something in Mexican pesos. They just have to convert their money based on the exchange rate on that day. With purchases made with credit cards, the exchange rate is calculated automatically. In Europe, many countries use the same currency. It is called the euro. This makes buying and selling easy.

When goods are sent out of a country to be sold in another nation, they are exported. When goods are brought into a country from another nation, they are imported. For example, in the United States, an imported car is one that comes from Korea; a domestic car is one that is built in the United States. The United States imports a lot of oil and exports a lot of grain. The farms in the Midwest help to feed the world through a network of railroads, highways, and shipping lanes.

The grain from the Midwest that will be exported must travel by train in a hopper car to a shipping dock on a river or ocean. When it arrives, the hopper car is emptied into the hold of a huge cargo ship. It takes many hopper cars to fill one cargo hold. After the ship moves across the ocean, the grain is unloaded in another seaport. Next, it travels by train or truck to a company that grinds it and makes it into tortillas, bread, cereal, or other foods. Then, it travels by truck to a store for people to purchase.

Teak is a type of wood that grows in the rain forests of Indonesia. Furniture is made from teak because it resists rot and is a pretty color. First, the teak trees must be chopped down. Then, the logs must be cut into lumber of a size that's easy to transport. The lumber travels to an ocean-going vessel. When it arrives in the United States, the teak is unloaded and put onto train cars. The train carries it to a furniture manufacturer. It makes teak boards into tables, chairs, benches, and desks. Trucks move the finished furniture to a store for people to buy.

When a nation imports more goods than it exports, there is a trade imbalance. This can cause economic problems. And because the world's economies are **interdependent**, a big problem in one may cause trouble in others. Americans have money invested in foreign corporations, and foreigners have money invested in U.S. companies. Economies are linked. If one economy went into a deep slump called a depression, it could have a domino effect on the other major economies. This means that they might all wind up in a depressed state.

Economies Are Connected

From the earliest civilization, people have traded with each other. Before money was invented, people used bartering, which was an inefficient system. What if you wanted something that someone else had, but you didn't have anything they wanted? Then, there was no way to make the trade.

Now, money is used for trade, and world banks keep track of how much one currency is worth compared to another on a daily basis. It is called an exchange rate. People in Japan can use yen to buy something in Mexican pesos. They just have to convert their money based on the exchange rate on that day. With purchases made with credit cards, the exchange rate is calculated automatically. In Europe, the use of one currency, the euro, makes buying and selling easy.

When goods are sent out of a country to be sold in another nation, they are exported, and when goods are brought into a country from another nation, they are imported. For example, in the United States, an imported car is one that comes from Korea; a domestic car is one that is built in the United States. The United States imports a lot of oil and exports a lot of grain. The farms in the Midwest help to feed the world through a network of railroads, highways, and shipping lanes.

The grain from the Midwest meant for export must travel by train in a hopper car to a shipping dock on a river or ocean. When it arrives, the hopper car is emptied into the hold of a huge cargo ship. It takes many hopper cars to fill one cargo hold. After the ship moves across the ocean, the grain is unloaded in another seaport. Next, it travels by train or truck to a company that grinds it and makes it into tortillas, bread, cereal, or other foods. Finally, it travels by truck to a store for people to purchase.

Teak is a type of wood that grows in the rain forests of Indonesia. Furniture is made from teak because it is a pretty color and resists decay. First, the teak trees must be chopped down and the logs must be cut into lumber of a size that's easy to transport. The lumber travels to an ocean-going vessel. When it arrives in the United States, the teak is unloaded, put onto train cars, and carried to a furniture manufacturer. The business transforms the teak boards into tables, chairs, benches, and desks. Trucks move the finished furniture to a store for people to buy.

When a nation imports more goods than it exports, there is a trade imbalance that can cause economic problems. And because the world's economies are **interdependent**, a problem in one may cause trouble in others. Americans have money invested in foreign corporations, and foreigners have money invested in U.S. companies. This links economies so that the fate of one affects them all. For example, if one economy went into a deep slump called a depression, it could have a domino effect on the other major economies in the world, and they might all wind up in a depressed state.

Economies Are Connected

Directions: Darken the best answer choice.

1. The currency unit used by the Japanese is called the
   - (A) peso.
   - (B) yen.
   - (C) dollar.
   - (D) euro.

2. The word **interdependent** means
   - (A) separate.
   - (B) unstable.
   - (C) in conflict.
   - (D) relying on each other.

3. When a foreign car is purchased in the United States, what happens last?
   - (A) The car travels by ship.
   - (B) The car travels by train.
   - (C) The car travels by truck to a dealership.
   - (D) A car is manufactured in Japan.

4. The United States economy is most apt to
   - (A) import oil and export teak.
   - (B) import oats and export clothing.
   - (C) import oil and export wheat.
   - (D) import wheat and export oil.

5. Brazilian cherry hardwood is used for floors. How does the lumber travel to factories in the United States?
   - (A) by ship and then train
   - (B) by plane and then train
   - (C) by ship and then plane
   - (D) by truck and then plane

6. During an economic depression, what would be *unlikely* to happen?
   - (A) People wouldn't buy as many goods.
   - (B) Many new stores would open.
   - (C) Companies would lay off workers.
   - (D) People and companies would go bankrupt.

Saving Earth One Bag at a Time

Have you ever heard of the Great Pacific Garbage Patch? It is a place in the Pacific Ocean where a large amount of trash circles in a current. This mass of debris is at least twice the size of Texas. It has been growing for more than fifty years. Oceanographers say that the garbage is 90 percent plastic. It weighs about one hundred million tons. The most common kind of trash floating there is plastic shopping bags. How did they all get there? All water flows downhill until it reaches the sea. Plastic bags that fall to the ground end up in water. That water ends up in the ocean.

The Garbage Patch is an environmental disaster. Ocean animals mistake pieces of plastic bags for food. They fill their stomachs with plastic. It does not pass through their guts as waste. The animals slowly starve to death. Yet scientists do not know of any way to clean up the mess. The only thing we can do is keep it from getting bigger.

What can you do to help? Stop using plastic bags! This would help our Earth in several ways. Like all plastic products, the bags are made with petroleum. The amount of petroleum used in fourteen plastic bags could drive a car a mile. Yet 380 billion plastic bags are thrown away each year just in the United States. That means millions of barrels of oil are used up in making the bags. And lots of those bags will end up in the Great Pacific Garbage Patch.

But using paper bags instead of plastic ones is *not* the answer. Making a paper bag releases 70 percent more global-warming gases than making a plastic bag. Eight out of every ten paper bags end up in landfills. Yet paper bags do not **biodegrade** there. Why? There is not enough oxygen. Without oxygen, bacteria cannot live. The paper bags need bacteria in order to decay. So paper bags, while useful for fifteen minutes, sit in landfills and take up space for hundreds of years.

Make a decision that you will never throw any bag into the trash. Each time you toss out a bag, you throw away natural resources. We cannot get them back. Plus, cities spend about 17 cents to dispose of each plastic or paper bag. This uses millions of tax dollars. That money could be spent in other ways. It might help the poor, make new jobs, or clean up the environment. New York City says that if each New Yorker used just one less bag per year, it would save $250,000!

What's the solution? When you run into the store to get just one or two items, tell the cashier, "I don't need a bag." If you do have your items bagged, return the bags to the store for recycling. Most stores have bins in which you can put used plastic or paper bags from any retailer. Some curbside recycling bins accept paper bags, too. Recycling bags uses less energy and materials than making them from scratch. Best of all, use bags made of fabric or canvas. Take these reusable bags into the store. Have your items put into them. You can use these bags many times before they need to be cleaned and hundreds of times before they'll need to be replaced. Most importantly, they will not end up in the sea.

Saving Earth One Bag at a Time

Have you ever heard of the Great Pacific Garbage Patch? It is a place in the Pacific Ocean where an enormous amount of trash circles in a current. This mass of debris, which is at least twice the size of Texas, has been forming for more than fifty years. Oceanographers estimate that the garbage is 90 percent plastic and weighs approximately one hundred million tons. The most common kind of trash floating there is plastic shopping bags. How did they all get there? Consider this: All water flows downhill until it reaches the sea. Plastic bags that fall to the ground eventually end up in water—water that ends up in the ocean.

This is an environmental disaster. Sea turtles, sea birds, and other ocean animals mistake pieces of plastic bags for food. They fill their stomachs with plastic that may not pass through their intestines as waste. The animals slowly starve to death. Yet scientists do not know of any way to clean up the mess. The only thing we can do is keep it from growing.

What can you do to help? Stop using plastic bags! This would help our Earth in multiple ways. Like all plastic products, the bags are made with petroleum. The amount of petroleum used in fourteen plastic bags could drive a car a mile. Yet 380 billion plastic bags are thrown away each year in the United States alone. That means millions of barrels of oil are used up for something that gets tossed out after a single use. Even worse, lots of those billions of bags will end up in the Great Pacific Garbage Patch.

But using paper bags instead of plastic ones is *not* the answer. Making a paper bag releases 70 percent more global-warming gases than making a plastic bag. Eight out of every ten paper bags end up in landfills. Yet paper bags do not **biodegrade** there. There is not enough oxygen. Without oxygen, the bacteria that would normally break down paper bags cannot live. So paper bags, while useful for fifteen minutes, sit in landfills taking up space for centuries.

Make a decision that you will never throw any bag into the trash. Each time you toss out a bag, you throw away natural resources that we cannot reclaim. Cities spend about 17 cents to dispose of each plastic or paper bag. This uses millions of tax dollars that could be spent in other ways, such as helping the poor, creating new jobs, or cleaning up the environment. In fact, New York City estimates that if each New Yorker used just one less bag per year, it would save the city $250,000!

What's the solution? When you run into the store to get just one or two items, tell the cashier, "I don't need a bag." If you do have your items bagged, return the paper or plastic bags to the store for recycling. Most stores have bins in which you can deposit used plastic or paper bags from any retailer. Some curbside recycling bins accept paper bags, too. Recycling bags uses fewer resources than creating them from scratch. Best of all, use bags made of fabric or canvas. Take these reusable bags into the store, and have your items put into them. You can use these bags many times before they need to be laundered and hundreds of times before they'll need replacement. Most importantly, they will never end up in the ocean.

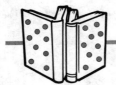

Saving Earth One Bag at a Time

Have you ever heard of the Great Pacific Garbage Patch? It is an enormous amount of trash rotating in a current in the Pacific Ocean. This enormous debris mass, which is at least twice the size of Texas, has been growing for more than fifty years. Oceanographers estimate that the garbage weighs approximately one hundred million tons and is 90 percent plastic. The most common kind of trash floating there is plastic shopping bags. How did they get there? All water flows downhill until it reaches the sea. Plastic bags that fall to the ground eventually end up in water that eventually ends up in the ocean.

The Great Pacific Garbage Patch is an environmental disaster unlike any other. Sea turtles, sea birds, and other ocean animals consume pieces of plastic bags, thinking they are food. The animals fill their stomachs with plastic that may not pass through their intestines, causing them to slowly starve to death. Unfortunately, scientists do not know of any way to clean up this mess, which means that the only thing we can do is keep it from growing even larger.

What can you do to help? Stop using plastic bags! This would help our Earth in multiple ways. Like all plastic products, the bags are made with petroleum, and the amount of petroleum in fourteen plastic bags could drive a car a mile. Yet 380 billion plastic bags are thrown away annually in the United States. Something that gets tossed out after a single use consumes millions of barrels of oil—a natural resource we are close to depleting. Even worse, many of those bags will end up in the Great Pacific Garbage Patch.

But using paper bags instead of plastic ones is *not* the answer. For one thing, making a paper bag releases 70 percent more global-warming gases than making a plastic bag. For another, 80 percent of paper bags end up in landfills where they do not **biodegrade** because there is not enough oxygen. Without oxygen, the bacteria that would normally break down paper bags cannot live. So paper bags, while useful for fifteen minutes, take up space in landfills for centuries.

Right now, make a decision that you will never throw any bag into the trash. Each time you toss out a bag, you throw away natural resources that we cannot reclaim. In addition, municipalities spend approximately 17 cents to dispose of each bag, using millions of tax dollars that could be spent to help the poor, create jobs, or clean up the environment. New York City estimates that if each New Yorker used just one less bag per year, it would save the city $250,000!

What's the solution? When you get just one or two items, tell the cashier, "I don't need a bag." If you do have your items bagged, return the paper or plastic bags to the store for recycling. Most stores have bins for you to deposit used plastic or paper bags from any retailer. Some curbside recycling bins also accept paper bags. Recycling bags uses fewer resources than creating them from scratch. Best of all, use bags made of fabric or canvas. Take these reusable bags into the store, and have your items packed in them. You can use these bags many times before they need to be laundered and hundreds of times before they'll need replacement. Most importantly, they will never end up in the ocean.

Saving Earth One Bag at a Time

Directions: Darken the best answer choice.

1. The Great Pacific Garbage Patch began forming when
   Ⓐ white settlers reached the West Coast.
   Ⓑ people redirected the currents in the Pacific Ocean.
   Ⓒ people began using paper bags.
   Ⓓ people began using plastic bags.

2. The word **biodegrade** means to
   Ⓐ shrink.
   Ⓑ last a long time.
   Ⓒ decompose.
   Ⓓ stay the same.

3. You get a plastic bag from the store. What is the best sequence of events?
   Ⓐ Take it home, empty it, and throw it into the trash.
   Ⓑ Take it home, empty it, and throw it on the ground.
   Ⓒ Take it home, empty it, and burn it in a woodstove.
   Ⓓ Take it home, empty it, and return it to the store's recycling bin.

4. In terms of the environment, the best type of bag to use is a
   Ⓐ fabric bag.
   Ⓑ paper bag.
   Ⓒ plastic bag.
   Ⓓ biodegradable bag.

5. Nine out of every ten items floating in the Great Pacific Garbage Patch are made of
   Ⓐ rubber.
   Ⓑ plastic.
   Ⓒ wood.
   Ⓓ leather.

6. What would you be most apt to see near the Great Pacific Garbage Patch?
   Ⓐ a sea turtle with a plastic six-pack ring around its neck
   Ⓑ seagulls nesting in paper bags
   Ⓒ flies buzzing around trash
   Ⓓ commercial fishing boats

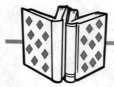

Humans Versus Natural Disasters

The Earth holds more than six billion humans. And not one of them lives in a 100-percent safe place. The American Midwest and other places with hot summers and miles of plains are ripe for tornadoes. Hurricanes are huge, spinning storms that form in the Atlantic Ocean. These storms form over warm seawater. They roar towards the people on shore with high winds, heavy rains, and tall waves. People living in the Ring of Fire face volcanic eruptions. The Ring of Fire is a large area. It forms a jagged "circle" in the Pacific Ocean. It runs along the coasts of several nations. All along this ring are more than 160 active volcanoes.

Humans have always looked for ways to protect themselves from natural disasters. Even with all our modern devices, we are no match for nature. But we do have some safeguards to improve our odds. For example, the invention of the Doppler radar is important. It lets weather scientists predict a tornado a few minutes before it touches down. They send warnings via radio and TV. That lets people go to their underground shelters to take cover. This has saved a lot of lives. Blizzards (snowstorms with dangerously low temperatures and high winds) can now be forecasted days ahead. Hurricanes and floods are predicted days in advance, too. This gives people time to **evacuate** the area. Evacuation routes are meant to help people to leave an area quickly. Yet there are not always enough roads out of a highly populated area.

Predicting a disaster isn't always enough. When Mount St. Helens erupted in May 1980, plenty of warning was given. The mountain rumbled and smoked for more than a month before it actually erupted. The people in the area were warned to leave. Some refused to do so. This was unwise. Fifty-seven people died.

Sometimes available precautions are not used. This happened in the Indian Ocean Tsunami of 2004. It hit Southeast Asian nations hard. Several huge waves drowned almost everyone in the area. Scientists know that sending people to high ground is the only thing to do once a tsunami forms. So they have put sensors on the Pacific Ocean floor. The sensors monitor the depth of the water above. They send data to a buoy. It sends the information to a satellite. From there, it is beamed to the Pacific Tsunami Warning Center in Hawaii. But there were none of these sensors in the Indian Ocean. Thus, when the undersea earthquake occurred in the Indian Ocean, no warning was sent. More than 220,000 people died from the tsunami.

At other times, precautions fail. Levees are strong concrete walls. Many were built to protect the low-lying city of New Orleans from the storm surges that come with a hurricane. These walls broke during Hurricane Katrina in August 2005. Water poured into the city. More than 1,800 people died. Although people had been told to flee, many had no way to get out of the city. Some people huddled on bridges or rooftops. Hundreds made it to the Superdome. This building was supposed to be a hurricane shelter. But it was not meant to hold so many people. They quickly ran out of food. The toilets stopped working. They suffered for days before help reached them.

Humans Versus Natural Disasters

There are more than six billion humans on Earth. And not one of them lives in a 100-percent safe place. Places with hot summers and miles of flat land—such as the American Midwest—are ripe for tornadoes. Hurricanes are gigantic, swirling storms that form in the Atlantic Ocean. They develop over warm ocean waters. They roar towards the people on shore with high winds, torrential rains, and towering waves. People living in the Ring of Fire face volcanic eruptions. The Ring of Fire is a large area. It forms a jagged "circle" in the Pacific Ocean and along the coasts of several nations. All along this ring are more than 160 active volcanoes.

People have always looked for ways to protect themselves from natural disasters. With all our inventions, we are no match for nature. But we do have safeguards to improve our odds. For example, the invention of the Doppler radar is important. It gives meteorologists the ability to predict a tornado a few minutes before it touches ground. They give warnings via radio and TV. That lets people rush to their underground shelters to take cover. This has saved countless lives. Blizzards are snowstorms with dangerously low temperatures and wind. They can now be forecast days ahead. Hurricanes and floods are predicted days in advance, too. This gives people time to **evacuate** the area. Evacuation routes are designed to help people to leave a populated area quickly. However, there are not always enough roads out of an area.

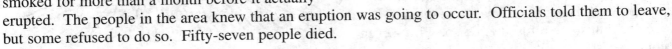

Predicting a disaster isn't always enough. When Mount St. Helens erupted in May 1980, plenty of warning was given. The mountain rumbled and smoked for more than a month before it actually erupted. The people in the area knew that an eruption was going to occur. Officials told them to leave, but some refused to do so. Fifty-seven people died.

Sometimes available precautions are not used. This happened in the Indian Ocean Tsunami of 2004 that devastated Southeast Asian nations. Several gigantic waves drowned almost everyone in the region. Scientists know that sending people to high ground is the only course of action once a tsunami forms. So they have placed sensors on the Pacific Ocean floor to monitor the depth of the water above. These sensors send data to a buoy that transmits the information to a satellite. From there, it is beamed to the Pacific Tsunami Warning Center in Hawaii. But there were none of these sensors in the Indian Ocean. Therefore, when the undersea earthquake occurred in the Indian Ocean, no warning was sent. More than 220,000 people died as a result.

At other times, precautions fail. Levees are concrete barriers. They were built to protect the low-lying city of New Orleans from the storm surges that come with a hurricane. These walls broke during Hurricane Katrina in August 2005. Water poured into the city, and more than 1,800 people perished. Although people had been warned to flee, many had no way to get out of the city. Some people survived by huddling on bridges or rooftops. Hundreds managed to make it to the Superdome. This building was designated as a hurricane shelter. But it was not meant to hold so many people. They quickly ran out of food, and the toilets stopped working. They suffered for days before help reached them.

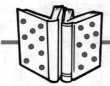

Humans Versus Natural Disasters

There are more than six billion humans on Earth, and not one of them lives in a 100-percent safe place. Places with hot summers and miles of flat land—such as the American Midwest—are ripe for tornadoes. Hurricanes are gigantic, swirling storms that develop over warm water in the Atlantic Ocean. They roar towards the people on shore with high winds, torrential rains, and towering waves. People living in the Ring of Fire face volcanic eruptions. The Ring of Fire is a large area that forms a jagged "circle" in the Pacific Ocean and along the coasts of several nations. All along this ring are more than 160 active volcanoes.

People have always looked for ways to protect themselves from natural disasters. Even with all our modern knowledge and inventions, we are no match for nature. Fortunately, we have created safeguards to improve our odds. For example, the invention of the Doppler radar is important because it allows meteorologists to predict a tornado a few minutes before it touches ground. They give warnings via radio and TV. That lets people rush to their underground shelters to take cover, saving countless lives. Blizzards are snowstorms with dangerously low temperatures and high winds. They can now be forecast days ahead. Hurricanes and floods are predicted days in advance, too. This gives people time to **evacuate** the area. Evacuation routes are designed to help people to leave a populated area quickly; however, there are not always enough roads out of an area.

Predicting a disaster isn't always enough. Before Mount St. Helens erupted in May 1980, the mountain rumbled and smoked for more than a month. The people in the area knew that an eruption would occur. Officials told them to evacuate, but some refused to do so. Fifty-seven people perished.

Sometimes available precautions are not utilized. This happened in the Indian Ocean Tsunami of 2004 that devastated Southeast Asian nations. Several gigantic waves drowned almost everyone in the region. Scientists know that once a tsunami forms, sending people to high ground is the only course of action. That's why there are sensors on the Pacific Ocean floor to monitor the depth of the water above. These sensors send data to a buoy that transmits the information to a satellite. From there, it is beamed to the Pacific Tsunami Warning Center in Hawaii. Unfortunately, there were no sensors placed in the Indian Ocean. Therefore, when the undersea earthquake occurred in the Indian Ocean, no warning was sent. Over 220,000 people died as a result.

At other times, precautions fail. Levees are concrete barriers built to protect the low-lying city of New Orleans from the storm surges that come with a hurricane. These walls broke during Hurricane Katrina in August 2005. Water poured into the city, and more than 1,800 people perished. Although people had been warned to flee, many had no way to leave the city. Some people survived by huddling on bridges or rooftops. Hundreds managed to make it to the Superdome, which had been designated as a hurricane shelter. But it was not meant to hold so many people. They quickly ran out of food, and the toilets stopped working. They suffered for days before help reached them.

Humans Versus Natural Disasters

Directions: Darken the best answer choice.

1. Humans have control over
   - Ⓐ tornadoes.
   - Ⓑ blizzards.
   - Ⓒ volcanic eruptions.
   - Ⓓ no natural disasters.

2. The word **evacuate** means to
   - Ⓐ leave an unsafe place.
   - Ⓑ rush to save someone.
   - Ⓒ protect homes from disaster.
   - Ⓓ practice disaster drills.

3. Which event happened third?
   - Ⓐ Mount St. Helens erupted and killed fifty-seven people.
   - Ⓑ The Great Flood of 1993 wrecked 10,000 homes in the Midwest.
   - Ⓒ Hurricane Katrina killed more than 1,800 people.
   - Ⓓ More than 220,000 people perished in a tsunami in Southeast Asia.

4. Mount St. Helens is part of the
   - Ⓐ Hurricane Katrina disaster.
   - Ⓑ tsunami warning system.
   - Ⓒ Doppler radar system.
   - Ⓓ Ring of Fire.

5. Levees are constructed to
   - Ⓐ direct water into a channel for hydropower.
   - Ⓑ hold back water from a populated area.
   - Ⓒ keep water in wetlands so that swamp life can thrive.
   - Ⓓ prevent hurricanes from forming over the ocean.

6. In 2006, tsunami warning buoys were installed for the first time in a new location. They were placed on the floor of the
   - Ⓐ Ring of Fire.
   - Ⓑ Pacific Ocean.
   - Ⓒ Indian Ocean.
   - Ⓓ Arctic Ocean.

That's Not Just Sunshine— It's Energy!

We know that in one hour more solar energy falls on Earth than the amount of energy used by the whole world in 2002. So why do we have problems getting enough energy? Can't the sun give us all we need? Yes, the sun can provide all the energy we would ever need. But we must find ways to capture it. And we need ways to store it. So far, we don't quite know how to capture or store it in an effective way. Scientists are working on these issues. Also, right now solar technology costs a lot. This is another problem. Scientists are working on that, too.

Today, most solar energy comes from Concentrating Solar Power systems. They use lenses or mirrors. They focus a large area of sunlight into one small beam. The concentrated ray of light heats a fluid. Water is the one used most. The heated water turns into steam. The steam spins turbines inside a power plant. This makes electric power. A lot of concentrating technologies are used. Three types are most often seen in the United States. They are the parabolic dish, the solar trough, and the solar power tower. Each one has a different way to follow the sun and focus its light. Some of these devices need a lot of space. Rather than take up land with the solar panels, some places put them on roofs.

Solar electricity can be made by photovoltaic, or solar, cells. Each of these cells has two silicon layers. When light shines on the top cell, electric current flows through a wire to the lower cell. All of these cells connect to a single wire. More electric power can be made with large cells and intense light. Solar cells can make electricity even on a cloudy day. Some sunlight passes through the clouds. The cells can generate much more on a sunny day.

Right now, solar cells are put in calculators and watches. They are used with some street lights, **navigation** buoys in rivers and bays, and in the small lamps along sidewalks in people's yards. In watches and calculators, the solar power gets used right away. For the others, it is stored in a battery. Then, it is used during darkness. Nearly every satellite we have put into orbit around Earth operates on solar cells. There is a steady supply of sunlight in outer space. There are no clouds and no nighttime.

Unless we can find a good way to store solar energy, there are limits to solar power. Due to Earth's tilt, less sunlight falls in the Northern and Southern Hemispheres during their winter months. That's just when people need the most energy to heat buildings. Also, people need energy twenty-four hours a day, but the sun does not shine at night. No solar energy can be made at night.

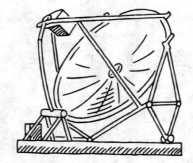

Parabolic Dish

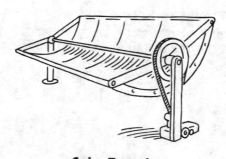

Solar Trough

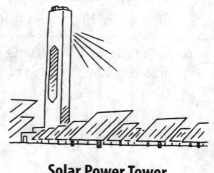

Solar Power Tower

That's Not Just Sunshine— It's Energy!

We know that more solar energy falls on Earth's surface each hour than the amount of energy used by the whole world during 2002. So why do we have problems getting enough energy? Can't the sun provide all we need? Actually, the sun can provide all of the energy we would ever need. But we must find ways to capture it and store it. So far, we don't quite know how to do that in an effective way. Scientists are working on this problem. Also, right now solar energy technology costs a lot. This is another problem that scientists are trying to fix.

Today, the most promising solar energy comes from Concentrating Solar Power systems. They use lenses or mirrors. They focus a large area of sunlight into a single beam. This concentrated ray of light heats a liquid, usually water. This makes steam. The steam spins turbines in a power plant, generating electricity. A lot of different concentrating technologies are used. The ones most often seen in the United States are the parabolic dish, the solar trough, and the solar power tower. Each one follows the sun and focuses its light in a different way. Some of these devices take up a lot of space. Rather than give up land with solar panels, some places have put them on roofs.

Solar electricity can be made by photovoltaic, or solar, cells. Each cell has two silicon layers. When light shines on the top cell, electric current flows through a wire to the lower cell. All of these cells then connect to a single wire. More electric power can be made with large cells and intense light. Electricity can be generated by solar cells even on a cloudy day. Some sunlight passes through the cloud cover. Much more can be generated on a sunny day.

Right now, solar cells are used in calculators and watches. They are used in some street lights, **navigation** buoys in rivers and bays, and the small lamps along sidewalks in people's yards. In watches and calculators, the solar power gets used right away. For the others, it is stored in a battery. Then, it is used during darkness. Nearly every satellite we have put into orbit around Earth operates on solar cells. There is a steady supply of sunlight in outer space. There are no clouds and no nighttime.

Unless we can find a good way to store solar energy, there are limits to solar power. Due to the Earth's tilt, less sunlight falls in the Northern and Southern Hemispheres during their winter months. That's just when people need the most energy to heat buildings. Also, people need energy twenty-four hours a day, but the sun does not shine at night. No solar energy can be made at night.

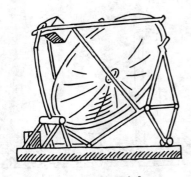

Parabolic Dish

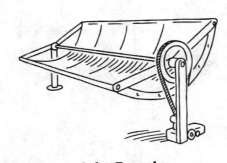

Solar Trough

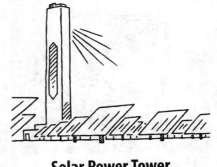

Solar Power Tower

That's Not Just Sunshine— It's Energy!

We know that more solar energy falls on Earth's surface each hour than the amount of energy used by the whole world during 2002. So why do we have problems getting enough energy? The sun could provide all of the energy we will ever need if we can capture it and store it. So far, we don't exactly know how to do that in an effective way. Scientists are working hard to solve this problem. Also, right now solar energy technology is expensive. This is another problem that scientists are trying to remedy.

Today, the most promising solar energy comes from Concentrating Solar Power systems. They use lenses or mirrors to focus a large area of sunlight into a single beam. This concentrated light ray heats a liquid, usually water, to create steam. This steam spins turbines in a power plant, generating electricity. Many different concentrating technologies are being used. The ones most commonly seen in the United States are the parabolic dish, the solar trough, and the solar power tower. Each one varies in the way in which it follows the sun and focuses its light. Some of these devices take up a lot of space. Rather than dedicate land to this use, some places have put the solar panels on rooftops.

Solar electricity can be generated in photovoltaic, or solar, cells. Each cell has two silicon layers. When light shines on the top cell, electric current flows through a wire to the lower cell. All of these cells then connect to a single wire. The amount generated increases with the size of the cells and the intensity of the light. Electricity can be generated by photovoltaic cells even on a cloudy day since there is still sunlight passing through the cloud cover. Of course, much more is generated on a sunny day.

Right now, solar cells are used in calculators, watches, some street lights, **navigation** buoys in waterways, and the small lamps lining walkways in people's yards. In watches and calculators, the solar energy is used right away. For the others, it is stored in a battery and then used during darkness. Nearly every satellite people have put into orbit around Earth operates on solar cells. There is a steady supply of sunlight in outer space since there are no clouds and no nighttime.

Unless we can find a good way to store solar energy, there are limits to solar power. Due to the way Earth tilts, less sunlight falls in the Northern and Southern Hemispheres during their winter months, which is just when people need the most energy for heat. Also, people need energy twenty-four hours a day, and the sun does not shine at night. No solar energy can be created at night.

Parabolic Dish

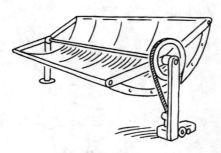

Solar Trough

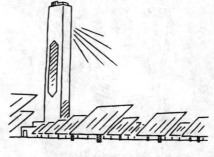

Solar Power Tower

That's Not Just Sunshine—
It's Energy!

Directions: Darken the best answer choice.

1. Every _____ more solar energy shines on Earth than the amount of energy people use worldwide in an entire year.
   Ⓐ minute
   Ⓑ hour
   Ⓒ day
   Ⓓ week

2. The word **navigation** means
   Ⓐ tsunami warning.
   Ⓑ expensive.
   Ⓒ ringing bells.
   Ⓓ directing the path.

3. In a Concentrated Solar Power system, which step happens third?
   Ⓐ A single beam of sunlight heats water.
   Ⓑ Steam gets generated.
   Ⓒ Turbines spin.
   Ⓓ Mirrors concentrate rays of sunlight.

4. The most solar energy can be collected
   Ⓐ at night.
   Ⓑ on a cloudy day.
   Ⓒ on a clear day.
   Ⓓ on a rainy day.

5. Photovoltaic cells are *not* currently used in
   Ⓐ computers.
   Ⓑ calculators.
   Ⓒ watches.
   Ⓓ yard lamps.

6. In the western part of the United States, there are "sun farms" with rows of solar collectors. Each farm's location is chosen primarily because
   Ⓐ the region is very flat.
   Ⓑ few wind storms typically occur in the region.
   Ⓒ the land is useless for other purposes.
   Ⓓ a lot of sunlight typically falls in the region.

Is Earth Overpopulated?

Earth's human population has grown a lot in the past one hundred years. In 1900, there were more than one billion people. By 2000, there were more than six billion. That is a big increase. It is due to sanitary living conditions and better healthcare, vaccines, and medicine. This means that people have clean water to drink and sewage and trash removal. While such things may not be available in poor countries, the developed nations of the world view them as standard. Some experts think that Earth cannot **sustain** this many people. Others disagree.

Overpopulation is when an organism's numbers exceed the carrying capacity of the environment. So the question is: are there enough natural resources available for all of the individuals? In some places where there is a lack of fresh water or farmland, there are too many people. That is why about 25,000 people starve to death daily.

The horror of people starving isn't the only problem. Too many people cause a lot of air, water, soil, and noise pollution. They use up natural resources too fast. They wreck ecosystems. Then, plants and animals become extinct. Plus, big population can lead to more crimes and even wars. Why? People fight for the limited resources.

Some modern nations have improved their carrying capacity. They use the best farming methods. This grows more food. They use nuclear power plants to make electric power. Then, they do not have to use fossil fuels. They desalinate seawater. This makes drinking water. Desalinating means distilling salt water. The water and salt separate. It leaves fresh water. It is costly to do.

CHINA

Population in an area grows when there are more births, fewer deaths, or a lot of immigrants. The world's population is rising because the number of babies born each year is greater than the number of people who die. That is why each year there are 725 million more people. At this rate, there will be eleven billion people by 2050. Can Earth keep that many people alive? No one knows.

At 1.3 billion, China has the world's biggest population.* Its leaders wanted to reduce the population. It would improve the quality of life. With fewer people, there are more resources for each one. In 1979, the Chinese government made a one-child policy. If a couple has more than one child, it will pay a fine. About 75 percent of the citizens agree with this. Yet this policy has caused problems. Some people do not want girls. They give them up, so they can try for a son. Luckily, people around the world adopt the unwanted babies. But now in China, there are 117 men for every 100 women. This means that a lot of men who want to marry can't find a wife.

*India may soon have the largest.

Is Earth Overpopulated?

There has been a huge growth in the human population during the past one hundred years. In 1900, there were more than one billion people on Earth. In 2000, Earth had more than six billion. That is a large increase. It is due in large part to sanitary living conditions and better healthcare, vaccines, and medicine. While these things may not be available in developing countries, the developed nations of the world view them as standard. Some experts feel that Earth cannot **sustain** this many people. Others disagree.

Overpopulation is a state where an organism's numbers exceed the carrying capacity of the environment. So the question is: are there enough natural resources available for all of the individuals? In many places in the world where there is a lack of farmland or fresh water, there are too many people. As a result, about 25,000 people starve to death each day.

The horror of people starving isn't the only problem with overpopulation. Too many people raise the levels of air, water, soil, and noise pollution. They use up natural resources and destroy ecosystems. This causes the extinction of plant and animal species. Plus, a large population can lead to more crimes and even wars as people compete for scarce resources.

Some modern nations have taken steps to improve their carrying capacity. They use the best farming methods. This produces the most food. They use nuclear power plants to generate electricity. Then, they do not have to rely on fossil fuels. They desalinate seawater to get enough drinking water. Desalinating means distilling salt water. This makes the water and salt separate. It leaves fresh water. It is costly to do.

CHINA

An area's population grows when there is an increase in births, a decrease in deaths, or a lot of new immigrants. The world's population is growing because the number of babies that are born each year is more than the number of people that die. The result is that each year there are 725 million more people. At this rate, by the year 2050, there will be eleven billion people. Can Earth keep that many people alive? No one knows for sure.

At 1.3 billion, China has the world's largest population.* Its leaders knew that the citizens' quality of life depended on reducing the population. With fewer people, there are more resources for each one.

So in 1979, the Chinese government made a one-child policy. The law states that if a couple has more than one child, it will pay a fine. About 75 percent of the citizens agree with the policy. Still, it has caused some problems. Many people do not want girls. They abandon them. Then, they can try for a son. Luckily, people around the world adopt the unwanted babies. But now in China, there are 117 men for every 100 women. A lot of men who want to marry can't find a wife.

*India may soon have the largest.

Is Earth Overpopulated?

No one questions the fact that there has been a huge growth in the human population during the past century. In 1900, there were over one billion people on Earth. In 2000, there were more than six billion. That is an enormous increase. It is due in large part to sanitary living conditions and better healthcare, vaccinations, and antibiotics. More people have clean water to drink and sewage and trash removal. While these things may not be available in impoverished countries, the developed nations of the world view them as standard. So what is under debate? It is whether or not the world is overpopulated. Some experts feel that Earth cannot **sustain** this many people. Others disagree.

Overpopulation is a state where an organism's numbers exceed the carrying capacity of the environment. That means there are not enough natural resources available for all the individuals in the population. In many places in the world where there is a lack of farmland or fresh water, there are too many people. As a result, about 25,000 people starve to death every day.

The horror of people starving isn't the only problem with overpopulation. Too many people increase the levels of air, water, soil, and noise pollution. They use up natural resources and destroy ecosystems. This results in the mass extinction of plant and animal species. Additionally, a large population can lead to an increased rate of crime and even war as people compete for scarce resources.

Some modern countries have taken steps to improve their carrying capacity. They use the best farming methods to produce the most food. They use nuclear power plants to generate electricity if they do not have access to fossil fuels. They desalinate seawater to provide enough drinking water. Desalinating means distilling salt water. This makes the salt separate from the water, leaving fresh water. It is expensive to do.

CHINA

An area's population grows when there is an increase in births, a decrease in deaths, or an influx of immigrants. The world's population is growing because the number of babies that are born each year is more than the number of people that die. This means that each year there are 725 million more people in the world. At this rate, by the year 2050, there will be eleven billion people on Earth. Can Earth keep that many people alive? Nobody knows for sure.

At 1.3 billion, China has the largest population on Earth.* Its leaders realized that the citizens' quality of life depended on reducing the population. With fewer people, there are more resources for each one. So in 1979, the Chinese government established a one-child policy. The law states that if a couple has more than one child, it will face fines. Approximately 75 percent of the citizens agree with the policy. Still, it has caused some problems. Many people do not want daughters. They abandon them, so they can try again for a son. Fortunately, people around the world adopt the unwanted babies. But in China, now there are 117 men for every 100 women. That means there are a lot of men who want to get married and can't find a spouse.

*India may soon overtake it.

Is Earth Overpopulated?

Directions: Darken the best answer choice.

1. Worldwide, about how many people starve to death each month?
   Ⓐ 25,000
   Ⓑ 750,000
   Ⓒ one million
   Ⓓ 725 million

2. The word **sustain** means
   Ⓐ use.
   Ⓑ help.
   Ⓒ support.
   Ⓓ reduce.

3. What happened second in Chinese history?
   Ⓐ The nation's population increased significantly.
   Ⓑ Citizens are fined if they have more than one child.
   Ⓒ The Chinese government adopted the one-child.
   Ⓓ There were too few resources for the number of people.

4. During one year in a nation, more people die than babies are born. What will definitely happen to its population?
   Ⓐ It will increase.
   Ⓑ It will decrease.
   Ⓒ It will be cut in half within ten years.
   Ⓓ It will be doubled within ten years.

5. You have a cage big enough for three female guinea pigs. If you add a fourth female guinea pig to the cage, you will have
   Ⓐ gone beyond the cage's carrying capacity.
   Ⓑ encouraged the guinea pigs to stop competing for food.
   Ⓒ improved conditions for the guinea pigs.
   Ⓓ destroyed the health of the guinea pigs.

6. Why is there a gender imbalance in China?
   Ⓐ Fewer males are born, and no one is sure why.
   Ⓑ Fewer females are born, and no one is sure why.
   Ⓒ Many males are adopted by people in other nations.
   Ⓓ Many females are adopted by people in other nations.

Ancient Chinese Inventions

Ancient China was an advanced society. Long ago, it had much more knowledge than other world civilizations at the time. Its people made a number of things hundreds of years before the people in Europe. Over time, Europeans took credit for many of these things. For example, the Chinese made the first magnetic compass. They made the first fishing reel. The next group to create a fishing reel did so 1,400 years later. Wheelbarrows, matches, and umbrellas all came from China.

The Western world did not even know about these things for a long time. Why? Few people went between Europe and China. It was a long trip. It was hard and dangerous. The Himalayas are the tallest mountain range on Earth. They stand between China and the rest of the continent. In 1274, an Italian named Marco Polo did go to China. He spent twenty-four years there. When he got home, he wrote a book. He told about all of the things he saw in China. But almost no one believed him!

The Chinese had a complex written language. They made separate symbols for each word. It took a long time to learn how to read and write. Only men called scholars could read and write. These men are the reason that the Chinese have the longest recorded history in the world. Much is known about their civilization for thousands of years in the past. For example, we know that the Chinese made the first mechanical clock. They made a basic instrument to measure earthquakes. They invented block printing. They knew how to make porcelain—what we call *china*—hundreds of years before anyone else.

Silk fabric, paper, and gunpowder are probably the best known of the Chinese inventions. The Chinese had paper as early as 105 CE. They started using paper money 700 years later. At about the same time, they invented gunpowder. However, in more recent times, the Chinese have not made as many advances.

No one is sure why, but around 1433, China entered a time of **isolation**. A Ming emperor made a choice. He decided China should not interact with the rest of the world. He ordered that the records of Zheng He, their great sea captain, be burned. Seaports closed to all but Asian traders. Things stayed this way until 1853. At that time, a British steamboat entered the waters between China and Japan. The people who saw the "smoking dragon" were shocked. They saw that their isolation had left them behind. They felt they would be vulnerable to attack by steamships.

How did this happen? During the 420 years of Chinese isolation, the rest of the nations in the world had kept trading with each other. People would see something they liked in another country. Then, they would try to make something just like it. Sometimes what they made was better. When people share ideas, the rate of change and growth is fast. Thus, people in Europe, Africa, and the Middle East made many advances, while China stayed nearly the same.

Ancient Chinese Inventions

Ancient China was an advanced society. At one time, it was far ahead of other world civilizations in its knowledge. Its people created a number of things hundreds of years before the people in Europe did. Over time, Europeans took credit for many of these things. For example, the Chinese actually made the first magnetic compass. They made the first fishing reel 1,400 years before anyone else. Wheelbarrows, matches, and umbrellas all came from China.

The Western world did not even know about these things for a long time. Why? Few people traveled between Europe and China. It was a long, hard, and dangerous trip. The Himalayas are the tallest mountain range on Earth. They stand between China and the rest of the continent. In 1274, an Italian named Marco Polo did go to China. He spent twenty-four years there. When he returned home, he wrote a book. He told about all of the amazing things he saw there. But almost no one in Europe believed him!

The Chinese had a complex written language with separate symbols for each word. It took a long time to learn how to read and write, and only scholars did so. These scholars are the reason that the Chinese have the longest recorded history in the world. Much is known about their civilization for thousands of years in the past. For example, we know that the Chinese created the first mechanical clock. They made a basic seismometer to measure earthquakes. They invented block printing. They made porcelain—what we call *china*—hundreds of years before anyone else knew how to make it.

Silk fabric, paper, and gunpowder are probably the best known of the Chinese inventions. The Chinese had paper as early as 105 CE. They started using the first paper money 700 years later. At about the same time, they invented gunpowder. However, in more recent times, the Chinese have not made as many advances.

No one is sure why, but around 1433, China entered a time of **isolation**. A Ming emperor decided China should not interact with the rest of the world. He ordered that all of the records of Zheng He, their great sea captain, be burned. Seaports closed to all but Asian traders. Things remained this way until 1853. At that time, a British steamboat entered the waters between China and Japan. The people were shocked by the "smoking dragon." They saw that their isolation had left them behind militarily.

How did this happen? During the 420 years of Chinese isolation, the rest of the nations in the world had kept trading with each other. This led to the free exchange of knowledge. People would see something they liked in another country and try to duplicate it in their own. When people share ideas, the rate of innovation moves fast. Thus, people in Europe, Africa, and the Middle East made many advances, while China remained nearly the same.

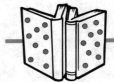

Ancient Chinese Inventions

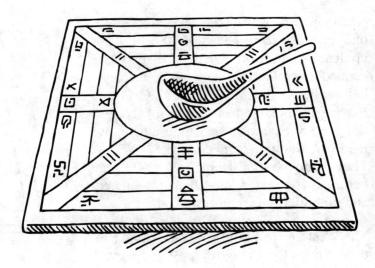

Ancient China was an advanced civilization. At one time, it was far ahead of other world civilizations in its knowledge. Its people created a number of things hundreds of years before the people in Europe did. Over time, Europeans have received the credit for many of these things. For example, the Chinese actually made the first magnetic compass. They made a fishing reel 1,400 years before anyone else. Wheelbarrows, matches, and umbrellas all came from China.

The Western world did not even know about these inventions for a long time. Why? Few people traveled between Europe and China. It was a long, hard, and dangerous trip. The Himalayas, the highest mountain range in the world, is a formidable obstacle that separates China from the rest of the continent. In 1274, an Italian named Marco Polo went to China. He spent twenty-four years there. When he returned home, he wrote a book about the amazing things he saw there. But almost no one in Europe believed him!

The Chinese had a complex written language with separate symbols for each word. It took a long time to learn how to read and write, and only scholars did so. These scholars are the reason that the Chinese have the longest recorded history in the world. This means much is known about their civilization for thousands of years in the past. For example, we know that the Chinese created the first mechanical clock and also a basic seismometer to measure earthquakes. They invented block printing and made porcelain—what we call *china*—hundreds of years before anyone else knew how to produce it.

Silk fabric, paper, and gunpowder are probably the best known of the Chinese inventions. The Chinese had paper as early as 105 CE. They started using the first paper money 700 years later, about the same time that they invented gunpowder. However, in more recent centuries, the Chinese have not made as many advances.

No one is sure why, but around 1433, China entered a time of **isolation**. A Ming emperor decided China should not interact with the rest of the world and destroyed all the records of their great sea captain Zheng He. Seaports closed to all but Asian traders. Things remained this way until 1853. At that time, a British steamboat entered the waters between China and Japan. When the shocked people saw the "smoking dragon," they realized that their isolation had left them vulnerable militarily.

How did this happen? During the 420 years of Chinese isolation, the rest of the nations in the world had continued to trade with each other. This led to the free exchange of knowledge, as it had for thousands of years. When people share ideas, the rate of innovation moves at a rapid pace. Thus, people in Europe, Africa, and the Middle East made discoveries, while China remained relatively unchanged.

Ancient Chinese Inventions

Directions: Darken the best answer choice.

1. Who demanded that China cut itself off from trading with the rest of the world?
   Ⓐ an emperor of the Ming dynasty
   Ⓑ Zheng He
   Ⓒ Marco Polo
   Ⓓ an emperor of the Song dynasty

2. The word **isolation** means
   Ⓐ joining together.
   Ⓑ great invention.
   Ⓒ financial hardship.
   Ⓓ separation from all others.

3. What happened first?
   Ⓐ The Chinese had paper money.
   Ⓑ Marco Polo visited China.
   Ⓒ The Chinese had paper.
   Ⓓ Zheng He's records were destroyed.

4. Which of these items was *not* invented by the Chinese?
   Ⓐ matches
   Ⓑ clay pottery
   Ⓒ mechanical clock
   Ⓓ silk fabric

5. Why did the Chinese realize that the "smoking dragon" was bad for their military?
   Ⓐ It looked so terrifying that it would make the Chinese soldiers too afraid to fight.
   Ⓑ It cost more to build a "smoking dragon" than a traditional Chinese ship.
   Ⓒ It could move faster and overtake the Chinese boats, which used sail power.
   Ⓓ It could destroy the whole nation of China before its army even had a chance to gather.

6. Which Chinese invention was made in response to a natural disaster?
   Ⓐ the seismometer
   Ⓑ the fishing reel
   Ⓒ gunpowder
   Ⓓ the wheelbarrow

The Seven Wonders of the Ancient World

Have you ever heard of the Seven Wonders of the Ancient World? It is a list of places that Greek tourists went to see long ago. It includes works from around the Mediterranean Sea. The oldest Wonder is the only one still standing. It is the Great Pyramid at Giza. The Egyptian pharaoh Khufu had it made about 2560 BCE. He was later buried in it. It is big. Its base covers thirteen acres. At its peak, it is as tall as a forty-story building. It took 100,000 workers more than twenty years to build.

King Nebuchadnezzar II had the Hanging Gardens of Babylon built in 600 BCE. It was a gift for his wife. It had stone terraces thirty stories high. Masses of colorful flowers were planted on each level. A lot of water was needed to keep the plants alive. A sprinkler system brought in water. It came from the Euphrates River.

Zeus was the most powerful Greek god. The Statue of Zeus was in the temple at Olympia. It was forty feet tall. The statue's eyes were big jewels. Its hair, beard, and clothes were coated with real gold. Phidia carved it from ivory about 435 BCE. He was the best artist in Greece at that time. It was ruined in a fire about 462 CE.

The beautiful Temple of Diana* was originally built in 800 BCE in Ephesus. Inside the temple stood a statue. She was the goddess of birth and children. More people went to this shrine than any other in ancient times. It was ruined by the Goths in 262 CE.

Queen Artemisia had the Tomb of King Mausolus built. It stood in Halicarnassus. The king had ruled Caria from 377 BCE to 353 BCE. His wife did not want him to be forgotten. The huge marble tomb had parts coated in gold. This monument added the word **mausoleum** to many languages. The king is still remembered.

The Colossus of Rhodes was a statue of Helios, the sun god. It stood with a raised torch in the harbor of Rhodes, a Greek island. Built in 280 BCE, it was over 110 feet tall. Its size was meant to scare off attackers. The people wanted invaders to sail on by! The statue was cast of bronze. The metal came from the melted weapons of the island's defeated enemies. But it stood just fifty-six years. In 224 BCE, an earthquake ruined it. Not even a trace of it remains. Today, the word *colossal* means huge.

The "newest" Wonder was the Lighthouse of Alexandria. Ptolemy Philadelphos built it in 280 BCE. It stood on the island of Pharos near Alexandria. This was the most useful Wonder. It helped to guide ships safely into the harbor. Made of marble, it was 407 feet tall. It had a fire that was always kept burning at the top. Mirrors behind the fire made the light seem brighter. Sea captains could see it from far away. An earthquake wrecked it in 1323 CE. To this day, it is the tallest lighthouse ever built.

The Seven Wonders did not all exist at the same time. Most of them were not shown in artwork. Pictures we see of them are what artists think they looked like based on old records.

*Since the Greeks called Diana "Artemis," it is sometimes called the Temple of Artemis.

The Seven Wonders
of the Ancient World

Have you ever heard of the Seven Wonders of the Ancient World? It is a list based on places that Greek tourists visited thousands of years ago. That's why it only includes works from around the Mediterranean Sea. The oldest Wonder—and the only one still standing—is the Great Pyramid at Giza. The Egyptian pharaoh Khufu had it built about 2560 BCE. He was later buried in it. It is so large that it covers thirteen acres. At its tallest point, it is as high as a forty-story building. It took 100,000 workers more than two decades to create.

King Nebuchadnezzar II had the Hanging Gardens of Babylon built in 600 BCE for his wife. It had stone terraces thirty stories high with masses of colorful flowers planted on every level. In this hot, dry land, a lot of water was needed to keep the flowers alive. A complex sprinkler system brought in water from the Euphrates River.

Zeus was the supreme Greek god. The Statue of Zeus in the temple at Olympia was forty feet tall. The statue's eyes were large jewels, and its hair, beard, and garments were gilded with real gold. Phidia carved it from ivory about 435 BCE. He was considered the greatest artist in Greece at that time. A fire ruined it around 462 CE.

The beautiful Temple of Diana* was originally built in 800 BCE in Ephesus. Inside the temple stood a statue of the goddess of fertility and childbirth. More people visited this shrine than any other in ancient times. It was destroyed by the invading Goths in 262 CE.

Queen Artemisia had the Tomb of King Mausolus erected at Halicarnassus. The king had ruled Caria from 377 BCE to 353 BCE. She did not want him to be forgotten. The gigantic marble tomb had parts coated in gold. Since this monument added the word **mausoleum** to many languages, the king is still remembered.

The Colossus of Rhodes was a statue of Helios, the sun god. It stood with a raised torch in the harbor of Rhodes, a Greek island. Built in 280 BCE, it was over 110 feet tall. Its immense size was meant to scare off attackers. The people wanted invaders to see their power and sail on by! The statue was cast of bronze that was obtained from the melted weapons of the island's defeated enemies. But it stood a mere fifty-six years. In 224 BCE, an earthquake ruined it, and not even a trace remains. Today, the word *colossal* means gigantic.

The "newest" Wonder was the Lighthouse of Alexandria built in 280 BCE by Ptolemy Philadelphos on the island of Pharos near Alexandria. It helped to guide ships safely into the harbor. Made of marble, it stood 407 feet tall, and at its top, a fire always burned. Mirrors behind the fire made the light seem brighter so that sea captains could see it from far away. It fell during an earthquake in 1323 CE. To this day, it remains the tallest lighthouse ever constructed.

The Seven Wonders did not all exist at the same time. Most of them were not captured in artwork. The pictures we see of them are what artists believe they looked like based on written descriptions.

*Since the Greeks called Diana "Artemis," it is sometimes called the Temple of Artemis.

The Seven Wonders of the Ancient World

Have you ever heard of the Seven Wonders of the Ancient World? It is a list based on places that Greek tourists visited thousands of years ago. This explains why it only includes works from around the Mediterranean Sea. The oldest Wonder—and the only one still standing—is the Great Pyramid at Giza, which the Egyptian pharaoh Khufu had built about 2560 BCE. He was later buried in it. It is so large that it covers thirteen acres, and at its tallest point, it is as high as a forty-story building. It took 100,000 workers more than two decades to construct.

King Nebuchadnezzar II had the Hanging Gardens of Babylon built in 600 BCE for his wife. It had stone terraces thirty stories high with masses of colorful flowers planted on every level. In this hot, dry region, a continuous supply of water was needed to keep the flowers alive. A complicated sprinkler system brought in water from the Euphrates River.

Zeus was the supreme Greek god. The Statue of Zeus in the temple at Olympia was forty feet tall. Phidia, considered the greatest Greek artist at that time, carved the statue from ivory about 435 BCE. Its eyes were large jewels, and its hair, beard, and garments were gilded with real gold. Fire destroyed it around 462 CE.

The beautiful Temple of Diana* was originally built in 800 BCE in Ephesus. Inside the temple stood a statue of the goddess of fertility and childbirth. More people visited this shrine than any other in ancient times. It was destroyed by the invading Goths in 262 CE.

Queen Artemisia had the Tomb of King Mausolus erected at Halicarnassus in honor of her husband, who had ruled Caria from 377 BCE to 353 BCE. She did not want the king to be forgotten. The gigantic marble tomb had parts coated in gold. Since this monument added the word **mausoleum** to multiple languages, the king is still remembered.

The Colossus of Rhodes was a statue of Helios, the sun god. It stood with a raised torch in the harbor of Rhodes, a Greek island. Built in 280 BCE, it was over 110 feet tall. Its immense size was meant to scare off attackers. The people wanted invaders to see their power and sail on by! The statue was cast of bronze that was obtained from the melted weapons of the island's defeated enemies. It stood a mere fifty-six years because in 224 BCE an earthquake ruined it, and not even a trace remains. Today, the word *colossal* means gigantic.

The "newest" Wonder was the Lighthouse of Alexandria built in 280 BCE by Ptolemy Philadelphos on the island of Pharos near Alexandria. This was the most useful Wonder, because it helped to guide ships safely into the harbor. Made of marble, it stood 407 feet tall and had a fire always burning at the top. Mirrors behind the fire made the light seem brighter so that sea captains could see it from far away. Although it fell during an earthquake in 1323 CE, it remains the tallest lighthouse ever constructed.

The Seven Wonders did not all exist at the same time. Most of them were not captured in artwork. Therefore, the pictures we see of them are what artists believe they looked like based on written descriptions.

*Since the Greeks called Diana "Artemis," it is sometimes called the Temple of Artemis.

The Seven Wonders of the Ancient World

Directions: Darken the best answer choice.

1. King Nebuchadnezzar II ordered the building of the
   - Ⓐ Colossus of Rhodes.
   - Ⓑ Statue of Zeus.
   - Ⓒ Hanging Gardens of Babylon.
   - Ⓓ Temple of Diana.

2. A **mausoleum** is a(n)
   - Ⓐ magnificent lighthouse.
   - Ⓑ aboveground tomb.
   - Ⓒ temple for worship.
   - Ⓓ kind of pyramid.

3. BCE means "Before the Common Era," and CE means in the "Common Era." Of these, which Wonder of the Ancient World was destroyed first?
   - Ⓐ the Statue of Zeus
   - Ⓑ the Colossus of Rhodes
   - Ⓒ the Lighthouse of Alexandria
   - Ⓓ the Temple of Diana

4. Which Ancient Wonder was built to show military might?
   - Ⓐ the Great Pyramid at Giza
   - Ⓑ the Temple of Diana
   - Ⓒ the Colossus of Rhodes
   - Ⓓ the Lighthouse of Alexandria

5. Which Ancient Wonder was made of marble?
   - Ⓐ the Statue of Zeus
   - Ⓑ the Colossus of Rhodes
   - Ⓒ the Hanging Gardens of Babylon
   - Ⓓ the Tomb of King Mausolus

6. Photographs exist of just one Ancient Wonder. It is the
   - Ⓐ Great Pyramid at Giza.
   - Ⓑ Tomb of King Mausolus.
   - Ⓒ Lighthouse of Alexandria.
   - Ⓓ Temple of Diana.

Germany and World War I

In 1871, the German Empire formed. Before that, the area had been small kingdoms. In 1890, Kaiser Wilhelm II took charge of the German Empire. Anything that Great Britain did, he wanted Germany to do better. He built factories until his nation went beyond Britain's industry and its ability to make steel. It was the first time any nation in Europe outdid Great Britain in industry. Also, Kaiser Wilhelm wanted the best navy. When the British built a naval vessel, he made one that was even better.

Wilhelm formed an alliance with Italy and Austria-Hungary. These nations agreed that if one of them got attacked, the others would come to its aid. On June 28, 1914, a Serbian killed an important man and his wife. The dead man's uncle was the leader of Austria-Hungary. Austria-Hungary declared war on Serbia. Russia said that it would defend Serbia. Wilhelm told them to back down. They did not. So on August 1, 1914, Germany declared war on Russia. Then, France joined Russia. It declared war on Germany.

Germany wanted to attack France. It marched troops through Belgium. On August 4, Great Britain declared war on Germany. This was the result of Germany invading Belgium. Italy didn't help Germany or Austria-Hungary as it had agreed to do. (Later in the war, Italy fought against Germany.)

There were four Central Powers. They were the German Empire, Austria-Hungary, the Ottoman Empire, and Bulgaria. At the start, it looked like they would win the war. Germany went through Belgium without a struggle. The Central Powers won a lot of the first battles, too. But then both sides dug trenches. Troops hid in these deep ditches and shot at their foes. After that, the fighting dragged on. It was rare that anyone gained ground.

Germany lost World War I. Why? Part of the reason was that the British invented the tank. The Germans had no weapon like it. Also, a German U-boat sank an ocean liner, the *Lusitania*. This happened on April 30, 1915. Americans died on the ship. After that, the United States entered the war. It sided with the Allies: Britain, France, and Russia. It sent a burst of new troops. By then, German troops were worn out.

Germany was hurt by World War I. France took over some of its land. Germany lost some of West Prussia when the nation of Poland was reestablished. Germany lost all of its colonies as well. This means that it lost about a million square miles in Africa and the Pacific.

But Germany's worst problem came from the Treaty of Versailles. It was signed on November 11, 1918. The Allies blamed Germany for the war. They said that the Germans had to pay for all of the damage. This demand for **reparations** ruined the German economy. It caused a severe depression. And it set the stage for World War II.

Germany and World War I

In 1871, the German Empire formed. Before that, the area had been a lot of small kingdoms. In 1890, Kaiser Wilhelm II was in charge of the German Empire. Anything that Great Britain did, he wanted Germany to do better. He built factories until his nation surpassed Britain's industry and its ability to make steel. This was the first time any European nation outdid Great Britain in industry. In addition, Kaiser Wilhelm wanted the best navy. Whenever the British built a naval vessel, he made one that was even better.

Wilhelm formed an alliance with Italy and Austria-Hungary. The nations agreed that if one of them were attacked, the others would come to its aid. On June 28, 1914, a Serbian killed Archduke Franz Ferdinand and his wife. The dead man's uncle was the emperor of Austria-Hungary. Austria-Hungary declared war on Serbia. The Russians said that they would defend Serbia. Wilhelm told them to back down. They refused. So on August 1, 1914, Germany declared war on Russia. Then, France joined Russia. It declared war on Germany.

Germany wanted to attack France. It marched soldiers through Belgium. On August 4, Great Britain declared war on Germany for invading Belgium. Italy didn't help Germany or Austria-Hungary as it had agreed to do. (Later in the war, Italy actually switched sides. It fought against Germany.)

The Central Powers were the German Empire, Austria-Hungary, the Ottoman Empire, and Bulgaria. At the start of the war, it looked like they would win. Germany marched through Belgium without resistance. The Central Powers won most of the first battles, too. But then both sides dug trenches. After that, the fighting dragged on without anyone gaining any ground.

Germany lost World War I due, at least in part, to the British invention of the tank. The Germans had no weapon like it. Also, a German U-boat sank an ocean liner, the *Lusitania*. This happened on April 30, 1915. This killed Americans. After that, the United States entered the war on the side of the Allies: Britain, France, and Russia. This burst of new troops came at a time when Germany's troops were worn out.

Germany was ruined by World War I. France took Alsace and Lorraine. The nation of Poland was reestablished by taking back some of West Prussia. Germany lost all of its colonial territories, too. This means that it lost about a million square miles in Africa and the Pacific.

But the worst burden for Germany was the Treaty of Versailles. It was signed on November 11, 1918. The Allies blamed the war on Germany. They said that the Germans had to pay for all of the destruction. This demand for **reparations** ruined the German economy. It caused a severe depression. Even worse, it laid the foundation for World War II.

Germany and World War I

The German Empire formed in 1871. For hundreds of years before that, the area had been a lot of small kingdoms run by princes. In 1890, Kaiser Wilhelm II took control of the German Empire. Anything that Great Britain did, Wilhelm wanted Germany to do better. He built factories until his nation surpassed Britain's industry and its ability to make steel. This was the first time any European nation outdid Great Britain in industry. In addition, Kaiser Wilhelm wanted to have the best navy. Whenever the British built a naval vessel, he made one that was even better.

Wilhelm formed an alliance with Italy and Austria-Hungary. The nations agreed that if one of them were attacked, the others would come to its aid. On June 28, 1914, a Serbian killed Archduke Franz Ferdinand and his wife. The dead man's uncle was the emperor of Austria-Hungary. Austria-Hungary declared war on Serbia. The Russians had agreed to defend Serbia. They got ready to fight. Wilhelm told them to back down. They refused. So on August 1, 1914, Germany declared war on Russia. Then, France joined Russia by declaring war on Germany.

Germany wanted to attack France. It marched soldiers through Belgium, a neutral nation. On August 4, Great Britain declared war on Germany for invading Belgium. Italy didn't help Germany or Austria-Hungary as it had agreed to do. (Later in the war, Italy actually switched sides and helped Germany's enemies.)

The Central Powers were the German Empire, Austria-Hungary, the Ottoman Empire, and Bulgaria. In the beginning of the war, it looked like they would win. After all, Germany marched through Belgium without any resistance. The Central Powers won most of the first battles. But then both sides dug trenches. After that, the fighting dragged on and on without anyone gaining any ground.

Germany lost World War I due, at least in part, to the British invention of the tank. The Germans had nothing like it. Also, a German U-boat sank the *Lusitania,* an ocean liner, on April 30, 1915. This killed American citizens. After that, the United States, which had been neutral, entered the war on the side of the Allies: Britain, France, and Russia. This replenishment of new troops came at a time when Germany's soldiers were exhausted.

Germany was devastated by World War I. It lost a lot of territory. France took Alsace and Lorraine. The nation of Poland was reestablished by reclaiming some of West Prussia. Germany also lost all of its colonial territories, which totaled about a million square miles in Africa and the Pacific.

But the worst burden for Germany was the Treaty of Versailles. It was signed on November 11, 1918. The Allies blamed the whole war on Germany. They insisted that the Germans pay for the destruction caused by the conflict. This demand for **reparations** caused a severe depression in Germany. Even worse, it laid the foundation for World War II.

Germany and World War I

Directions: Darken the best answer choice.

1. What country did Germany lose as the result of World War I?
   - Ⓐ Belgium
   - Ⓑ Bulgaria
   - Ⓒ France
   - Ⓓ Poland

2. The word **reparations** means
   - Ⓐ money paid to cover damages.
   - Ⓑ loaning money to rebuild.
   - Ⓒ reversing a trend.
   - Ⓓ destruction.

3. What happened second?
   - Ⓐ France took over some of Germany's land.
   - Ⓑ Germany marched through Belgium.
   - Ⓒ Relatives of the Austria-Hungary leader were killed.
   - Ⓓ Italy joined the Allies against Germany.

4. The purpose of the Treaty of Versailles was to
   - Ⓐ help the German economy recover after World War I.
   - Ⓑ restore land to Germany that had been taken by its enemies.
   - Ⓒ punish Germany for its aggression.
   - Ⓓ make Germany join the Allies.

5. The European nations' alliances for mutual defense
   - Ⓐ helped World War I to end quickly.
   - Ⓑ reduced the number of dead and wounded soldiers.
   - Ⓒ turned over the nation of Belgium to Germany without a fight.
   - Ⓓ made many of them get involved in the fighting.

6. Picture the trenches of World War I. What do the soldiers have in the trenches?
   - Ⓐ guns
   - Ⓑ tanks
   - Ⓒ nuclear warheads
   - Ⓓ planes

The Curse of the Bambino

Do you know what a curse is? The Boston Red Sox baseball team does. For eighty-six years, this team felt like it had been cursed. The players and coaches felt unlucky. They could not win a championship title, no matter how hard they tried.

It was called the Curse of the Bambino. It was named after a baseball player. His name was Babe "the Bambino" Ruth. Ruth was a pitcher and outfielder for the Boston Red Sox from 1914–1919. During this time, he helped his team win three World Series titles. The Red Sox played at Fenway Park. Everyone thought the Red Sox was the best-known baseball team in America. They had a total of five out of fifteen World Series wins. But in January of 1920, all of this changed.

The owner of the Red Sox sold Ruth to the New York Yankees. He did this in order to pay the mortgage on Fenway Park and the making of a Broadway play. This is when the curse began. Soon, the Red Sox began to lose their success. On the other hand, the Yankees, an **unrecognized** team, began to gain fame. Ruth himself also had great success with the Yankees. In his first season with them, he broke the single-season home run record he had once set with the Red Sox. He also had a .847 slugging percentage.

Unfortunately, Boston's luck continued to fade. They didn't play in a World Series game until 1946. And they lost the title to the St. Louis Cardinals. In that same span of time, the Yankees played in fourteen World Series and won ten of them. The Yankees had once become the most successful baseball team in America.

The Red Sox players were frustrated. The fans were getting restless. The Red Sox wanted the fame they once had. They wondered if the curse could be broken. Many attempts at breaking the curse were made. One fan put a Red Sox cap on top of Mt. Everest and burned a Yankees cap at its base camp. Others hired exorcists to "cleanse" Fenway Park. But perhaps the most noted attempt appeared on Storrow Drive. There, a street sign stood that had once informed drivers of a "Reverse Curve." However, because of the curse, the sign was spray-painted to say "Reverse the Curse."

Do you think the sign worked? On October 27, 2004, after eighty-six years of heartache and disappointment, the Red Sox defeated the St. Louis Cardinals to win the World Series. The curse was broken at last! After this historic event, the Red Sox went on to win the 2007 World Series as well. With these two World Series wins on the record, the Red Sox are proving themselves to be a solid and strong baseball team once again.

The Curse of the Bambino

Do you know what a curse is? The Boston Red Sox baseball team does. For eighty-six years, this team felt like it had been cursed. The players and coaches felt unlucky because they could not win a championship title, no matter how hard they tried.

The Curse of the Bambino was named after a famous baseball player, Babe "the Bambino" Ruth. Ruth was a pitcher and outfielder for the Boston Red Sox from 1914–1919. During this time, he helped his team win three World Series titles. The Red Sox played at Fenway Park. The Red Sox were one of the most successful baseball teams, with a total of five out of fifteen World Series wins. But in January of 1920, all of this changed.

The owner of the Red Sox decided to sell Ruth to the New York Yankees in order to pay the mortgage on Fenway Park and finance the production of a Broadway play. This is when the curse began. Suddenly, the Red Sox began to lose their success. On the other hand, the Yankees, an **unrecognized** team, began to gain fame. Ruth himself also had significant success with the Yankees. In his first season with them, he broke the single-season home run record he had previously set with the Red Sox. He also had a .847 slugging percentage.

Unfortunately, Boston's luck continued to fade. They didn't play in a World Series game until 1946 and then lost the title to the St. Louis Cardinals. In that same span of time, the Yankees played in fourteen World Series and won ten of them. The Yankees had become the most well-known and most successful baseball team in America.

The Red Sox players were frustrated, and the fans were getting restless. The Red Sox longed for the fame they once had, and they wondered if the curse could be broken. Many attempts at breaking the curse were made. One fan placed a Red Sox cap atop Mt. Everest and burned a Yankees cap at its base camp. Others hired exorcists to "purify" Fenway Park. But perhaps the most noted attempt appeared on Storrow Drive. There, a street sign stood that had once informed drivers of a "Reverse Curve." However, because of the curse, the sign was spray-painted to say "Reverse the Curse."

Do you think the sign worked? On October 27, 2004, after eighty-six years of heartache and disappointment, the Red Sox defeated the St. Louis Cardinals to win the World Series. The curse was broken at last! After this historic event, the Red Sox went on to win the 2007 World Series as well. And with these two World Series wins on the record, the Red Sox are proving themselves to be a solid and strong baseball team once again.

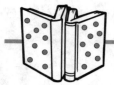

The Curse of the Bambino

Do you know what a curse is? The Boston Red Sox baseball team does. For eighty-six years, this team assumed it had been cursed. The players and coaches felt doomed and unlucky because they could not win a championship title, no matter their effort.

The Curse of the Bambino was named after a reputable baseball player, Babe "the Bambino" Ruth. Ruth was a pitcher and outfielder for the Boston Red Sox from 1914–1919. During this time, he helped his team win three World Series titles. The Red Sox played at Fenway Park. The Red Sox were one of the most successful baseball teams, with a total of five out of fifteen World Series wins. But in January of 1920, all of this changed.

The owner of the Red Sox decided to sell Ruth to the New York Yankees in order to pay the mortgage on Fenway Park and finance the production of a Broadway play. This is when the curse began. Suddenly, the Red Sox saw a decline in their success, while the Yankees, an **unrecognized** team, accrued much fame. Ruth himself also had significant prosperity with the Yankees. In his first season with them, he broke the single-season home run record he had previously established with the Red Sox and had a .847 slugging percentage.

Unfortunately, Boston's luck continued to vanish. They didn't play in a World Series game until 1946 and then lost the title to the St. Louis Cardinals. In that same span of time, the Yankees played in fourteen World Series and won ten of them. The Yankees had become the most acknowledged and noteworthy baseball team in America.

The Red Sox players were disheartened, and the fans were getting agitated. The Red Sox yearned for the fame they once had, and they wondered if the curse could be broken. Many attempts at breaking the curse were made. One fan deposited a Red Sox cap atop Mt. Everest and set aflame a Yankees cap at its base camp. Others enlisted exorcists to "purify" Fenway Park. But perhaps the most noted venture appeared on Storrow Drive. There, a street sign was erected that had once informed drivers of a "Reverse Curve." However, because of the curse, the sign was spray-painted to declare "Reverse the Curse."

Do you think the sign was effective? On October 27, 2004, after eighty-six years of heartache and distress, the Red Sox defeated the St. Louis Cardinals to win the World Series. The curse was broken at last! After this historic occasion, the Red Sox went on to win the 2007 World Series as well. With these two World Series wins on the record, the Red Sox are proving themselves to be a capable and tenacious baseball team once again.

The Curse of the Bambino

Directions: Darken the best answer choice.

1. Who was "the Bambino"?
   - Ⓐ the coach of the St. Louis Cardinals
   - Ⓑ the coach of the Boston Red Sox
   - Ⓒ a player on the Boston Red Sox
   - Ⓓ the name of a Broadway play

2. The word **unrecognized** means
   - Ⓐ in need of repair.
   - Ⓑ unhappy.
   - Ⓒ surprising.
   - Ⓓ not famous.

3. Which event happened second?
   - Ⓐ Babe "the Bambino" Ruth broke the single-season home run record for the second time.
   - Ⓑ Babe "the Bambino" Ruth was sold to the New York Yankees.
   - Ⓒ The Red Sox defeated the St. Louis Cardinals to win the World Series.
   - Ⓓ A fan put a Red Sox cap on top of Mt. Everest.

4. What happened after the Red Sox's owner sold Babe Ruth to the Yankees?
   - Ⓐ The Red Sox put a curse on the Yankees.
   - Ⓑ Everyone saw a decline in Babe Ruth's success.
   - Ⓒ The Red Sox continued to win World Series titles.
   - Ⓓ The owner paid the mortgage on Fenway Park.

5. Why did fans attempt to break the curse?
   - Ⓐ They were excited.
   - Ⓑ They wanted the Red Sox to win a World Series.
   - Ⓒ They were tired of their team's success.
   - Ⓓ They missed Babe Ruth.

6. Which area of the baseball stadium did Babe Ruth rarely visit?
   - Ⓐ the seats
   - Ⓑ the pitcher's mound
   - Ⓒ the outfield
   - Ⓓ home plate

Barack Obama, 44th President of the United States

The date was January 20, 2009. A record-breaking number of people stood huddled in the cold. They were at the Capitol building in Washington, D.C. They wanted to watch the inauguration of the first African American president of the United States. Barack Obama put his hand on the Bible. He was sworn in as the 44th president. Cheers went up from the crowd.

When he was a child, few would have guessed that Obama would one day be the U.S. president. His parents had met and married in college. His mother, Ann Durham, was from Kansas. His father, also named Barack Obama, was from Kenya. Their marriage did not last long. The elder Obama returned to Africa. Obama only met him once when he was ten years old. Ann married a man from Indonesia. She took her young son to live there. Obama lived and went to school in Indonesia for a few years. Then, his mother's second marriage fell apart.

Obama grew up in Hawaii. He went to a private school. He got a very good education. When he was older, he went to college. After he graduated, he got a job. He was a community organizer. A community organizer is a person who gets people together to talk about problems and find solutions. Once the people have formed a group, the organizer finds the person(s) in the government to address the group's **grievances**. Obama did this job in Chicago. This city is in Illinois. He had some minor successes. Yet, he felt like he wasn't doing enough to improve the lives of the poor. He thought that being in politics would let him make the changes he longed to see happen. So he left his job. He went to Harvard University. He studied law.

As a student there, Obama received an honor. He was chosen to be president of the *Harvard Law Review*. He was the first African American to hold this position. The *Harvard Law Review* is a journal. It has pieces about legal issues. Some are written by professors. Others are written by students. Becoming president practically guaranteed Obama a career as a high-paid lawyer. But he had other plans. He married Michelle Robinson in 1992. She was another lawyer. Just four years later, he quit practicing law. He became an Illinois state senator. He served in that role for eight years. At the same time, he taught law part-time at a college in Chicago.

Barack Obama

Then, Obama set his sights higher. He ran for a seat in the U.S. Senate. He won and took the oath of office in January 2005. But he did not serve out his four-year term. Just two years later, he decided to run for the highest office in the nation. He had to step down as senator in November 2008 when he won the U.S. presidency.

The people of Illinois were sad to lose their senator. But they were proud, too. Once again, a man who represented their state would lead the nation. What other president came from Illinois? Abraham Lincoln. If Lincoln were still alive, he would've been proud when Obama said, "There's not a black America and white America and Latino America and Asian America. There's the United States of America."

Barack Obama, 44th President of the United States

The date was January 20, 2009. A record-breaking number of people stood huddled in the cold in Washington, D.C. They were gathered at the Capitol building. They were there to watch the inauguration of the first African American president of the United States. Cheers went up from the crowd after Barack Obama put his hand on the Bible and was sworn in as the 44th president.

When he was a child, few would have guessed that Obama would one day be the president of the most powerful nation in the world. His parents had met and married while in college. His mother, Ann Durham, was from Kansas. His father, also named Barack Obama, was from Kenya. Their marriage did not last long, and the elder Obama returned to Africa. Obama only met him once when he was ten years old. Ann married a man from Indonesia and took her young son to live there. Obama lived and attended school in Indonesia for several years. Then, his mother's second marriage fell apart.

Obama grew up in Hawaii. He attended a private school and got an excellent education. When he was old enough, he went to college. After he graduated, he worked as a community organizer. A community organizer is someone who gets people together to discuss problems and potential solutions. Once the people have formed a group, the organizer finds the right person(s) in the government to address the group's **grievances**. Obama worked in Chicago, Illinois. He had some minor successes. Even so, he felt like he wasn't making enough of an impact in the lives of the poor. He believed that being in politics would enable him to make the reforms he longed to see happen. So he left his job. He went to Harvard University to earn a law degree.

While a student there, Obama received an honor. He was chosen to be president of the *Harvard Law Review*. He was the first African American to hold this position. The *Harvard Law Review* is a journal. It has articles about legal issues. They are written by professors and students. Becoming president practically guaranteed Obama a career as a high-paid lawyer. But he had other plans. He married Michelle Robinson, another lawyer, in 1992. Just four years later, he quit practicing law to be an Illinois state senator. He served in that role for eight years. At the same time, he taught law part-time at a college in Chicago.

Barack Obama

Then, Obama set his sights higher. He ran for a seat in the U.S. Senate and won. He took the oath of office in January 2005. But he did not serve out his four-year term. Just two years later, he announced that he was running for the highest office in the nation. He had to step down as senator in November 2008 when he won the U.S. presidency.

The citizens of Illinois were sad to lose their senator. But they were proud that once again a man who represented their state would lead the nation. What other president came from Illinois? Abraham Lincoln. If Lincoln were alive today, he would've been proud when Obama said, "There's not a black America and white America and Latino America and Asian America; there's the United States of America."

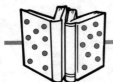

Barack Obama, 44th President of the United States

The date was January 20, 2009. A record-breaking number of people stood huddled in the cold; they gathered at the Capitol building in Washington, D.C. They were there to watch the inauguration of the first African American president of the United States. Cheers went up from the crowd after Barack Obama put his hand on the Bible and was sworn in as the 44th president.

When he was a child, few would have guessed that Obama would one day be the president of the most powerful nation in the world. His parents had met and married while in college. His mother, Ann Durham, was from Kansas, and his father, also named Barack Obama, was from Kenya. Their marriage did not last long, and the elder Obama returned to Africa. Obama only met him once when he was ten years old. Ann married a man from Indonesia and took her young son to live there. Obama lived and attended school in Indonesia for several years until his mother's second marriage fell apart.

Obama grew up in Hawaii. He attended a private school where he received an excellent education. When he grew up, he went to college. After he graduated, he worked as a community organizer. A community organizer gets people together to discuss problems and potential solutions. Once the people form a group, the organizer finds the right person(s) in the government to address the group's **grievances**. Obama worked in Chicago, Illinois, and had some minor successes. Even so, he felt like he wasn't making enough of an impact in the lives of the poor. He believed that being in politics would enable him to make the reforms he longed to see happen. So he left his job and went to Harvard University to earn a law degree.

While a student there, Obama received an honor. He was chosen to be president of the *Harvard Law Review*. He was the first African American to hold this position. The *Harvard Law Review* is a journal about legal issues. The articles are written by both students and professors. Becoming president practically guaranteed Obama a career as a high-paid lawyer, but he had other plans. He married Michelle Robinson, another lawyer, in 1992. Just four years later, he quit practicing law to be an Illinois state senator. He served in that role for eight years. He simultaneously taught law part-time at a college in Chicago.

Barack Obama

Then, Obama set his sights higher. He ran for a seat in the U.S. Senate and won. He took the oath of office in January 2005, but he did not serve out his four-year term. Just two years later, he announced that he was running for the highest office in the nation. When he won the U.S. presidency in November 2008, he had to step down as senator.

The citizens of Illinois were sad to lose their senator, yet they were proud that once again a man who represented their state would lead the nation. What other president came from Illinois? Abraham Lincoln. If Lincoln were alive today, he would've been proud when Obama said, "There's not a black America and white America and Latino America and Asian America; there's the United States of America."

Barack Obama, 44th President of the United States

Directions: Darken the best answer choice.

1. Where did Obama grow up?
    Ⓐ in Kenya
    Ⓑ in Hawaii
    Ⓒ in Illinois
    Ⓓ in Indonesia

2. The word **grievances** means
    Ⓐ worries.
    Ⓑ complaints.
    Ⓒ tax problems.
    Ⓓ diseases.

3. Of these events, which happened second?
    Ⓐ Obama earned a law degree.
    Ⓑ Obama was a state senator.
    Ⓒ Obama was a community organizer.
    Ⓓ Obama was a U.S. senator.

4. Reread the last line. Why would Abraham Lincoln have been pleased with what Obama said?
    Ⓐ Lincoln came from Illinois, too.
    Ⓑ Lincoln also graduated from Harvard University.
    Ⓒ Lincoln had fought to keep the United States as one nation.
    Ⓓ Lincoln had black, Latino, and Asian cabinet members.

5. With which of these issues would a community organizer help?
    Ⓐ arresting the people who sell drugs
    Ⓑ enrolling children in public school
    Ⓒ shoveling snow from sidewalks
    Ⓓ finding ways to connect the unemployed with jobs

6. Why did Obama resign from being a U.S. senator?
    Ⓐ He wanted to return to his position as president of the *Harvard Law Review*.
    Ⓑ He was asked to be a community organizer and felt he could make a greater impact in that role.
    Ⓒ He wanted to go back to teaching law.
    Ⓓ He could not hold two political positions at the same time.

Robots

Perhaps you have seen the movie *Wall-E*. It makes robots seem almost human. But robots are not like us. That's what makes them so useful. Many factories use robots. Robots do the dull, repetitive tasks that people dislike. They do these jobs faster and with fewer mistakes than humans, too. For example, a robot can fasten a screw on each object on an assembly line. The robot never gets bored doing this. It never gets sick and has to stay home. A robot can work in conditions that would be too hot or cold or dangerous for a human. For instance, robots can fix pipes deep underwater. They can work where the water pressure is too high for a human.

The word robot came from *robota*. That is a Czech word. It means **drudgery**. Most robots stay in one spot. The ones in factories often have an arm. It has a tool on the end. The tool may be a screwdriver, a drill, or some other item. Some do not have tools but do lifting or sorting tasks. Robots cost manufacturers a lot. So engineers are working to make robots that can do different jobs. They can have their program changed. Let's say that a robot drills a hole in metal. It has a drill at the end of its arm. It is programmed to drill to a set depth. After a few years, the factory does not need the drilling robot. Now, the need is for a robot that sprays paint. A flexible robot will be able to have its program changed. Its drill can be traded for a spray gun. Then, it will paint instead of drill.

A few robots have artificial intelligence. That's because a human programmed the computer within the robot. This means it can make choices. Sensors on the robot take readings. Then the computer program within the robot uses the readings. It makes a decision. For example, a robot's job may be to pick up something breakable. The sensors keep the robot from holding it too tightly. Engineers want to design artificial intelligence robots to do dangerous tasks without human command. Such a robot might be able to control a tank during a war. The U.S. military already uses remote-controlled planes in war zones. There is no pilot inside the plane. These aircraft are directed by humans. The people sit at a control panel far from the

battle. If one of these planes gets shot down, it is a costly loss. But preventing the loss of a pilot is much better.

Robotics is the engineering field devoted to making robots. In addition to the typical robots, scientists have made some complex ones. They cost a lot of money because they can move around. They often have electronic sensors. They may carry cameras. These robots operate from a combination of stored instructions, sensor feedback, and remote controls. They have visited places where no human has ever been. Such robots have already gone to the surface of Mars. They have gone to Earth's ocean floors, too. We have learned a lot from the information these robots have gathered for us.

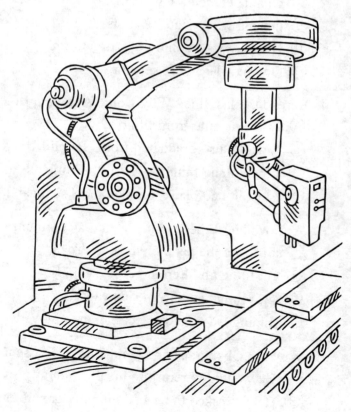

Robots

Perhaps you have seen the movie *Wall-E*. It makes robots seem almost human. But robots are definitely not like us. In fact, that's what makes them useful. Many factories rely on robots. Robots do the dull, repetitive tasks that people don't like. They perform these jobs faster and with greater accuracy than humans, too. For example, a robot can fasten a screw on each object on an assembly line. The robot never gets bored doing the same thing. It never gets sick and has to stay home from work. In addition, a robot can function in conditions that would be too hot or cold or dangerous for a human. For instance, robots can repair underwater pipes where the water pressure is too high for a human.

The word robot came from *robota*, a Czech word. It means **drudgery**. Most robots stay in one spot all the time. The ones in factories usually have an arm with a tool attached to the end. The tool may be a screwdriver, a drill, or something else. Some do not have tools but do lifting or sorting instead. Robots cost manufacturers a lot of money. So engineers are working to make robots that can do different jobs by having their programming modified. Let's say that a robot drills a hole in metal. It has a drill at the end of its mechanical arm. It is programmed to drill to a certain depth. But after a few years, the factory does not need the drilling robot. Now, the need is for a robot that can spray paint. A flexible robot will be able to have its program changed. Its drill can be traded for a spray gun. Then, it will do the new job.

A few robots have artificial intelligence. That's because a human programmed the computer inside the robot so that it can make choices. Sensors on the robot take readings. Then, the computer program within the robot interprets the readings in order to make a decision. For instance, a robot's job may be to pick up something breakable. The sensors keep the robot from grasping it too tightly. Engineers are trying to design artificial intelligence robots to do dangerous tasks without human direction. Such a robot might be able to operate a tank during a war. The U.S. military already uses remote-controlled airplanes that have no pilots. These aircraft are controlled by humans. The people are sitting at a control panel far from the battlefield. If one of these planes gets shot down, it is an expensive loss. But preventing the loss of a pilot is more important.

The engineering field devoted to improving robots is called robotics. In addition to the typical robots, scientists have made some very complex and expensive ones. They can move around. They often have electronic sensors. They may carry video cameras. These robots operate from a combination of stored instructions, sensor feedback, and remote controls. They have boldly gone where no human has ever been. Such robots have already been successfully sent to the surface of Mars. They have gone to Earth's ocean floors, too. We've learned a great deal from the information these robots have gathered for us.

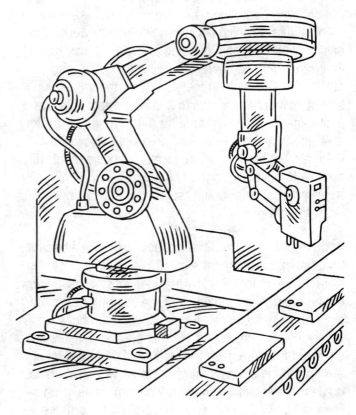

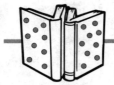

Robots

Perhaps you have seen the movie *Wall-E*, which makes robots seem almost human. But robots are definitely not like humans, and that's what makes them useful. Many factories use robots to do the dull, repetitive tasks that people don't enjoy. Robots can perform such jobs faster and with greater accuracy than humans, too. For example, a robot may fasten a screw on each object that comes through an assembly line. It never gets distracted or daydreams and misses a screw. It never gets bored doing the same thing or gets sick and has to stay home from work. Plus, a robot can work in conditions that would be too hot or cold or dangerous for a human, such as repairing underwater pipes where the water pressure is high.

The word robot came from *robota*, a Czech word that means **drudgery**. Most robots stay in one spot all the time. The ones in factories usually have an arm with a tool affixed to the end. The tool may be a screwdriver or a drill—whatever is needed. Some do not have tools but do lifting or sorting tasks. Robots are expensive for manufacturers, which is why engineers are working to design robots capable of doing different jobs by having their programming changed. Let's say that a robot currently drills a hole in metal. It uses the drill at the end of its mechanical arm to make a certain size hole to a certain depth. However, after a few years, the factory no longer needs as many drilling robots. Now, the need is for a robot that can spray paint. A flexible robot will be able to have its program changed and the drill removed from its arm and replaced with a spray gun in order to do the new task.

Some robots have artificial intelligence. That's because a human programmed the computer within the robot so that it appears to "think" by making decisions. Sensors on the robot take readings that the computer program uses to make a choice. For instance, if a robot's job is to pick up something that's breakable, the sensors keep the robot from grasping the item too tightly. Engineers are now trying to design artificial intelligence robots to do dangerous tasks without any human supervision. Such a robot might be able to operate a tank during a war. The U.S. military is already using remote-controlled airplanes without pilots. These aircraft are controlled by humans sitting at a control panel far away from the battlefield. If one of these planes gets shot down, it is an expensive loss. But preventing the loss of a pilot is more important.

The engineering field devoted to designing robots is called robotics. In addition to the typical robot, scientists have made some very sophisticated and expensive ones that can move around. They have electronic sensors for touch and may carry video cameras. These robots operate from a combination of stored instructions, sensor feedback, and remote controls. By successfully exploring the surface of Mars and Earth's ocean floors, they have boldly gone where no human has ever been. We have learned amazing things from the data these robots have collected and sent back to us.

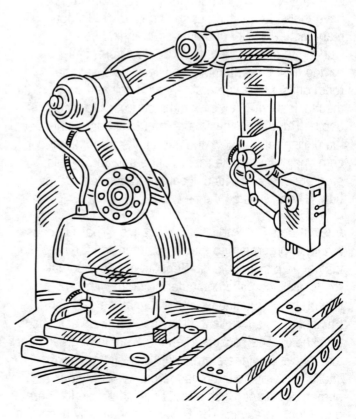

Robots

Directions: Darken the best answer choice.

1. Only a robot with artificial intelligence can
   Ⓐ have sensors.
   Ⓑ make choices.
   Ⓒ be programmed to do a repetitive task.
   Ⓓ operate in places that are dangerous for humans.

2. The word **drudgery** refers to a(n)
   Ⓐ boring job.
   Ⓑ low-paying job.
   Ⓒ unpaid job.
   Ⓓ exciting job.

3. Which kind of robots are engineers currently working on?
   Ⓐ robots with flexible programming
   Ⓑ robots that do the same thing over and over
   Ⓒ robots with artificial intelligence
   Ⓓ robots that explore the surface of Mars

4. A factory has a robot that uses a drill. The foreman wants the robot to use a staple gun instead. Which is true?
   Ⓐ The robot needs cameras installed.
   Ⓑ The robot must be a flexible one that can have its program modified.
   Ⓒ The robot must be a very complex one that costs a lot of money.
   Ⓓ The robot needs remote control sensors installed.

5. The majority of robots
   Ⓐ stay in the same place all the time.
   Ⓑ have been to Mars.
   Ⓒ have artificial intelligence.
   Ⓓ operate in battlefields.

6. Picture a person operating a remote-controlled aircraft in a war zone. How does the person give the aircraft commands?
   Ⓐ by cell phone
   Ⓑ by text messaging
   Ⓒ by computer
   Ⓓ by television

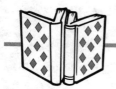

SEARCH Biographynow.com   [Paul Newman]   **GO**

Paul Newman (1925–2008) Superstar and Humanitarian

Paul Newman was a movie superstar. He was also a racecar driver, a **humanitarian**, and a devoted spouse. Paul was born in 1925 in Cleveland. By the age of seven, he showed an interest in acting. After high school, he served in World War II. He was in the South Pacific. When he came home, he went to college. There, he had several roles in the school's plays. Upon graduation, he went to Chicago. He worked in a theater group called the Woodstock Players. There, he met and married actress Jackie Witte. Soon, they had a son named Scott. The couple decided to take a risk. Paul would try for an acting career. He went to Yale. He started to work on a graduate degree in drama. While studying there, he had two daughters. In 1953, he moved to New York City. He had a starring role in a Broadway play. A movie executive saw Paul act. He hired him to play a role in a movie. But the movie bombed. It was so bad that Paul bought a full-page ad apologizing for his performance!

Yet Paul didn't give up. He kept appearing in plays. He took roles in movies. He hoped to have another chance to be a movie star. Then, when he was thirty-one years old, Newman's big break came. He was praised for his role in the movie *Somebody Up There Likes Me*. After that, movie scripts poured in. He could pick his roles. In 1958, he and his wife got divorced. Then, he married Joanne Woodward. She was an actress he had met five years earlier. Their marriage lasted fifty years. They had three daughters.

In 1969, Paul took racecar-driving lessons. He did it to get ready for a role. He found that he loved racing. He started to race in his spare time. In 1977, he began entering professional races. He even won a few. For a while, everything seemed to be going his way. Then, in 1978, his son Scott died of a drug overdose. To deal with his grief, Paul began the Scott Newman Foundation. It helps to stop drug and alcohol abuse. It was his first nonprofit organization. Paul became devoted to helping others.

For Christmas gifts in 1980, Paul and his friend A. E. Hotchner made homemade salad dressing. The pair enjoyed doing this. They created Newman's Own® in 1982. All of the company's profits went to charities. The company now makes much more than salad dressings. It has popcorn, spaghetti sauce, and cookies. Newman's Own was a big success.

At the time of his death in 2008, Newman's Own had already given away a lot of money. It had donated more than $250 million to charities. Some of this money funded the Hole in the Wall Camps. They are another of Paul's creations. There are now eight of these camps around the world. Children with life-threatening illnesses can go to one of them for a free vacation.

All actors hope to earn an Academy Award. It is called an Oscar. Paul was nominated ten times for an Oscar. He won twice. Now, he is gone. But Paul's charities and Newman's Own live on. They keep doing good for others. Paul Newman was a superstar in more ways than one.

Paul Newman

SEARCH Biographynow.com | Paul Newman | GO

Paul Newman (1925–2008) Superstar and Humanitarian

Paul Newman was a movie superstar. He was also a racecar driver, a **humanitarian**, and a devoted spouse. He was born in 1925 in Cleveland. By the age of seven, he showed an interest in acting. After high school, he served in the South Pacific during World War II. When he returned home, he went to college and played several roles in the school's productions. Upon graduation, he went to Chicago to work in a theater group called the Woodstock Players. There, he met and married actress Jackie Witte. Soon, they had a son named Scott. The couple decided to take a risk and have Paul pursue an acting career. He began work on a graduate degree in drama at Yale. While studying there, he had two daughters. In 1953, he moved to New York City and had a starring role in a Broadway play. A Warner Brothers executive saw Paul act and hired him to play a role in a movie. But the movie bombed. It was so bad that Paul bought a full-page ad apologizing to moviegoers for his performance!

Yet Paul didn't give up. He kept appearing in plays and taking roles in movies in the hopes of having a second chance at stardom. Then, when he was thirty-one years old, Newman's big break came. His role in the movie *Somebody Up There Likes Me* won him accolades, and suddenly movie scripts started pouring in. He had his choice of roles. In 1958, he and his wife divorced. He then married Joanne Woodward, an actress he had met five years earlier. Their marriage lasted fifty years. They had three daughters.

In 1969, Paul took racecar-driving lessons to prepare for a role. Discovering a passion for racing, he began to race in his spare time. In 1977, he began entering professional races and even won a few. For a while, everything seemed to be going his way. Then, in 1978, his son Scott died of a drug overdose. To deal with his grief, Paul began the Scott Newman Foundation to prevent drug and alcohol abuse. It was his first nonprofit organization devoted to helping others.

For Christmas 1980, Paul and his friend A. E. Hotchner prepared homemade salad dressing to give for gifts. The pair enjoyed doing this so much that they created Newman's Own® in 1982. All of the company's profits went to charities. The company now makes much more than salad dressings, including popcorn, spaghetti sauce, and cookies. Newman's Own was a huge success.

Paul Newman

At the time of his death in 2008, Newman's Own had donated more than $250 million to charities. Some of this money has gone to fund the Hole in the Wall Camps, another of Paul's creations. There are now eight of these camps worldwide. Children with deadly illnesses can go to one of them for a free vacation.

All actors hope to earn an Academy Award called an Oscar. Paul was nominated ten times for an Oscar, winning twice. Although he is gone, Paul's charities and Newman's Own continue doing good for others. Paul Newman was a superstar in more ways than one.

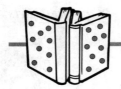

Web Page

SEARCH Biographynow.com | Paul Newman | **GO**

Paul Newman (1925–2008) Superstar and Humanitarian

Paul Newman was a movie superstar, a racing champion, a **humanitarian**, and a devoted spouse. Born in 1925 in Cleveland, by the age of seven, he showed an interest in acting. After high school, he served in the South Pacific during World War II. When he returned home, he went to college and played several roles in the school's productions. Upon graduation, he went to Chicago to work in a theater group called the Woodstock Players. There, he met and married actress Jackie Witte, and soon they had a son named Scott. The couple decided to take a risk and have Paul pursue an acting career. He began work on a graduate degree in drama at Yale. While studying there, he had two daughters. In 1953, he moved to New York City and had a starring role in a Broadway play where a Warner Brothers executive saw him act and offered him a movie role. Unfortunately, the movie bombed; in fact, it was so bad that Paul bought a full-page ad apologizing to moviegoers for his performance!

Yet Paul didn't give up. He kept appearing in plays and taking movie and television roles in the hopes of having a second chance at stardom. Then, when he was thirty-one years old, Newman's big break came when his role in the movie *Somebody Up There Likes Me* won him accolades. Suddenly, movie scripts started pouring in, and he had his choice of roles. In 1958, he and his wife divorced. He then married Joanne Woodward, an actress he had met five years earlier. Their marriage lasted fifty years and produced three daughters.

In 1969, when Paul took racecar-driving lessons to prepare for a role, he discovered his passion for racing. He began to race in his spare time, and in 1977, he began entering professional races and won a championship. Everything seemed to be going his way until his son Scott died of a drug overdose in 1978. To deal with his grief, Paul began the Scott Newman Foundation to prevent drug and alcohol abuse. It was his first nonprofit organization devoted to helping others.

For Christmas gifts in 1980, Paul and his friend A. E. Hotchner prepared homemade salad dressing. The pair enjoyed doing this so much that they created Newman's Own® in 1982 to market their salad dressing. All of the company's profits went to charities. Besides salad dressings, the company now sells more products, including popcorn, spaghetti sauce, and cookies. Newman's Own was an enormous success.

At the time of his death in 2008, Newman's Own had donated more than $250 million to charities. Some of this money has gone to fund the Hole in the Wall Camps, another of Paul's creations, where children with deadly illnesses can go for a free vacation. There are now eight of these camps worldwide.

All actors hope to earn an Academy Award called an Oscar. Paul was nominated ten times for an Oscar, winning twice. Although he is gone, Paul's charities and Newman's Own continue doing good for others, proving that Paul Newman was a superstar in more ways than one.

Paul Newman

Paul Newman

Directions: **Darken the best answer choice.**

1. Paul cofounded Newman's Own® with
   - Ⓐ his son, Scott Newman.
   - Ⓑ his wife, Joanne Woodward.
   - Ⓒ his friend, A. E. Hotchner.
   - Ⓓ two of his daughters.

2. The word **humanitarian** means a person who
   - Ⓐ is an actor.
   - Ⓑ helps other people.
   - Ⓒ wins car races.
   - Ⓓ starts a business.

3. Which event occurred first?
   - Ⓐ Paul and his first wife got a divorce.
   - Ⓑ Paul started a business called Newman's Own.
   - Ⓒ Paul won a professional car race.
   - Ⓓ Paul felt embarrassed for being in a lousy movie.

4. What is the purpose of the Hole in the Wall Camps?
   - Ⓐ to give seriously ill children a chance to have fun
   - Ⓑ to help children whose parents abuse drugs
   - Ⓒ to give seriously ill children a chance to have the surgery they need
   - Ⓓ to house children who have escaped from war-torn areas

5. What prompted Paul Newman to start his first charity?
   - Ⓐ His son died of an overdose.
   - Ⓑ His daughter died of cancer.
   - Ⓒ His wife was seriously injured in a car crash.
   - Ⓓ He had a grandchild with a life-threatening illness.

6. By 2008, Newman's Own had donated to charities a
   - Ⓐ quarter of a million dollars.
   - Ⓑ half a million dollars.
   - Ⓒ quarter of a billion dollars.
   - Ⓓ half a billion dollars.

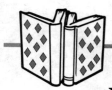

Visit the Bizarre Winchester Mansion
San Jose, California

William Winchester was the inventor of the Winchester repeating rifle. When he died in 1881, he left his wife Sarah a lot of money. She held a séance in order to speak to her dead husband. Instead, she heard spirits. They told her that she must move to the West and build a new home. They said she must work nonstop to expand her house. If she stopped, she would die. For the next thirty-eight years, she hired laborers. They worked twenty-four hours a day to make the most **convoluted** and strange house on Earth. Work ended the day after she died.

During her lifetime, Mrs. Winchester would not let anyone inside. She even refused President Theodore Roosevelt. Now, you can be one of the few to tour this amazing house.

Opens at 9 a.m., 364 Days a Year
Closed Christmas Day

Tour Type	Adults (15–64)	Seniors (65+)	Children (6–14)
Grand Tour (includes mansion, attics, and basements)	$31	$28	Children (10–14) $28 Our insurance prohibits children under ten from this tour
Mansion Only Tour	$26	$23	$20 Children under five free with adult admission

The Winchester House by the Numbers

Stories: 7 prior to the 1906 earthquake; now 4
Rooms: 750 prior to 1906 earthquake; now 160
Bedrooms: 40
Kitchens: 6
Ballrooms: 2 (one complete and one was under construction)
Staircases: 40
Doors: 950 (not including cabinet doors)
Skylights: 52
Fireplaces: 47 (gas, wood, or coal burning)
Gallons of paint required to paint exterior: Over 20,000
Construction dates: 1884 until September 5, 1922 (38 continuous years!)
Total cost: $5.5 million

Visit the Bizarre Winchester Mansion
San Jose, California

William Winchester, the inventor of the Winchester repeating rifle, died in 1881. He left his wife Sarah a fortune. She held a séance. She did it in order to speak to her dead husband. Instead, she claimed that spirits spoke to her. They stated that unless she moved to the West, built a home, and never stopped expanding on it, she would die. So for the next thirty-eight years, she had laborers work twenty-four hours a day to create the most elaborate, **convoluted**, and bizarre house on Earth. Work ceased the day after she died.

During her lifetime, Mrs. Winchester refused entrance to anyone. She wouldn't even let President Theodore Roosevelt inside. Now, you can be one of the fortunate few to tour this amazing mansion.

Opens at 9 a.m., 364 Days a Year
Closed Christmas Day

Tour Type	Adults (15–64)	Seniors (65+)	Children (6–14)
Grand Tour (includes mansion, attics, and basements)	$31	$28	Children (10–14) $28 Our insurance prohibits children under ten from this tour
Mansion Only Tour	$26	$23	$20 Children under five free with adult admission

The Winchester House by the Numbers

Stories: 7 prior to the 1906 earthquake; now 4
Rooms: 750 prior to 1906 earthquake; now 160
Bedrooms: 40
Kitchens: 6
Ballrooms: 2 (one complete and one was under construction)
Staircases: 40
Doors: 950 (not including cabinet doors)
Skylights: 52
Fireplaces: 47 (gas, wood, or coal burning)
Gallons of paint required to paint exterior: Over 20,000
Construction dates: 1884 until September 5, 1922 (38 continuous years!)
Total cost: $5.5 million

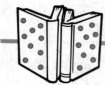

Visit the Bizarre Winchester Mansion
San Jose, California

In 1881, William Winchester, the inventor of the Winchester repeating rifle, died. He left his wife Sarah a fortune. She held a séance in order to speak to her dead husband. Instead, she claimed that spirits told her that unless she moved to the West, built a home, and continuously expanded on it, she would die. For the next thirty-eight years, she had laborers work twenty-four hours a day to create the most elaborate, **convoluted**, and bizarre house on Earth. Work ceased the day after she died.

During her lifetime, Mrs. Winchester refused entrance to anyone, even President Theodore Roosevelt. Now, you can be one of the fortunate few to tour this architectural marvel.

Opens at 9 a.m., 364 Days a Year
Closed Christmas Day

Tour Type	Adults (15–64)	Seniors (65+)	Children (6–14)
Grand Tour (includes mansion, attics, and basements)	$31	$28	Children (10–14) $28 Our insurance prohibits children under ten from this tour
Mansion Only Tour	$26	$23	$20 Children under five free with adult admission

The Winchester House by the Numbers

Stories: 7 prior to the 1906 earthquake; now 4
Rooms: 750 prior to 1906 earthquake; now 160
Bedrooms: 40
Kitchens: 6
Ballrooms: 2 (one complete and one was under construction)
Staircases: 40
Doors: 950 (not including cabinet doors)
Skylights: 52
Fireplaces: 47 (gas, wood, or coal burning)
Gallons of paint required to paint exterior: Over 20,000
Construction dates: 1884 until September 5, 1922 (38 continuous years!)
Total cost: $5.5 million

Visit the Bizarre Winchester Mansion

Directions: Darken the best answer choice.

1. What was the purpose of Sarah Winchester's séance?
   - Ⓐ She wanted to know how to build the Winchester repeating rifle.
   - Ⓑ She wanted to talk to President Theodore Roosevelt.
   - Ⓒ She wanted to talk to her parents.
   - Ⓓ She wanted to talk to William.

2. The word **convoluted** means
   - Ⓐ dangerous.
   - Ⓑ complicated.
   - Ⓒ largest.
   - Ⓓ most expensive.

3. What happened second?
   - Ⓐ Sarah told a U.S. president to stay out of her home.
   - Ⓑ Sarah claimed that spirits told her to expand her home.
   - Ⓒ William Winchester died.
   - Ⓓ Laborers worked on the Winchester Mansion.

4. What happened to the house in 1906?
   - Ⓐ Construction of the house began.
   - Ⓑ Construction on the house ended.
   - Ⓒ It was partially destroyed by an earthquake.
   - Ⓓ It was completely destroyed by an earthquake.

5. Read about the Grand Tour. Why do you think children under ten are not allowed on it?
   - Ⓐ Children have been lost in the mansion and never found.
   - Ⓑ The mansion is too dangerous for the kids.
   - Ⓒ The mansion's attics and basements might be too dangerous for them.
   - Ⓓ Sarah Winchester insisted that children under ten could never enter her home.

6. On what date would it be impossible for you to tour the Winchester Mansion?
   - Ⓐ January 1
   - Ⓑ July 4
   - Ⓒ October 31
   - Ⓓ December 25

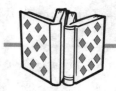
Public Service Advertisement

VIZ-A-PHONE*

Deaf or Hearing Impaired? Yes, You Can Use the Telephone!

Is it hard for you to hear on the phone? Have you given up on using the phone? Let Viz-a-Phone change your life! It's a new, FREE service in our state. It is meant for deaf and hearing-impaired persons who like to speak during calls.

How Does Viz-a-Phone Work?

Using a computer, open your Viz-a-Phone account. You can use any phone. Dial a toll-free number to reach a Viz-a-Phone operator. You can call 24 hours a day, 365 days a year. Your computer will verify the operator connection. Dial the number of the person or business you wish to call. When the person answers, the operator will "caption" the call. The operator will key in each word spoken by the person you have called. These captions appear on your computer screen. It is just like captions for TV programs.

You can get Spanish captions, too. How? Just register for a Spanish operator when you set up your free Viz-a-Phone account.

How Can You Get Started?

1. Your computer must have a modem or be connected to DSL service.
2. Download the free Viz-a-Phone software. It is available at this URL: *http://viz-a-phone.org/download*. Follow the easy, step-by-step instructions on our Web site.
3. Open a free Viz-a-Phone account.
4. Use any phone to dial the Viz-a-Phone service at 123-456-7890. Follow the on-screen instructions. This will **activate** your account. Now, you can make your first call!

Benefits:

- Viz-a-Phone gives you visual support on your computer screen. Your phone gives you auditory support. You may understand phone calls better than ever!

- You choose the caption size, color, and font. This is helpful if you need a large font due to vision problems.

- You can save and print the conversation captions.

The captioning service is funded by the Telecommunications Relay Service. It is part of Title IV of the Americans with Disabilities Act (ADA).

*Note: The specific product shown in this advertisement is fictional; however, there are similar products available. You can search for these online.

Public Service Advertisement

VIZ-A-PHONE*

Deaf or Hearing Impaired? Yes, You Can Use the Telephone!

Is it hard for you to follow phone conversations? Have you given up on using the phone? Then, Viz-a-Phone can change your life! It's a new, FREE, statewide service. It's meant to help deaf and hearing-impaired persons who like to speak during calls.

How Does Viz-a-Phone Work?

Using a computer, open your Viz-a-Phone account. You can use any phone to dial a toll-free number to reach a Viz-a-Phone operator. Operators are available 24 hours a day, 365 days a year. Once your computer verifies the operator connection, dial the number of the person or business you wish to call. When the person answers, the operator will "caption" the call. The operator will key in each word spoken by the person you have called. The captions appear on your computer screen. This is just like the closed captions for television programs.

Spanish captions are available, too. Just register for a Spanish operator when you set up your free Viz-a-Phone account.

How Can You Get Started?

1. Your computer must have a modem or be connected to DSL service.
2. Download the free Viz-a-Phone software. It is available at this URL: *http://viz-a-phone.org/download*. Follow the easy, step-by-step instructions on our Web site.
3. Open a free Viz-a-Phone account.
4. Use any phone to dial the Viz-a-Phone service at 123-456-7890. Follow the on-screen instructions. This will **activate** your account. Now, you're ready to make your first call!

Benefits:

- You get auditory support from your phone and visual support from your computer.
- You choose the size, color, and font of the captions. This is very helpful if you need a large font due to poor vision.
- You can save and print the conversation captions.

The captioning service is funded by the Telecommunications Relay Service. It is part of Title IV of the Americans with Disabilities Act (ADA).

*Note: The specific product shown in this advertisement is fictional; however, there are similar products available. You can search for these online.

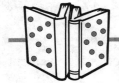

Public Service Advertisement

VIZ-A-PHONE*

Deaf or Hearing Impaired? Yes, You Can Use the Telephone!

Do you have difficulty understanding conversations on the phone? Have you given up on using the phone? Then, Viz-a-Phone will change your life! It's a new, FREE, statewide service designed for deaf and hard-of-hearing individuals who may have residual hearing loss or who would like to speak during calls.

How Does Viz-a-Phone Work?

Through your computer, open your Viz-a-Phone account. You can use any phone to dial a toll-free number to contact a Viz-a-Phone operator. Operators are available 24 hours a day, 365 days a year. Once your computer verifies the connection to the operator, dial the number of the person you wish to call. When the person answers, the operator will begin "captioning" the call. Each word spoken by the party you have called is keyed in by the operator. These captions will appear on your computer screen just like closed captions for television programs appear on a television screen.

Spanish captioning is available, too. Simply register for a Spanish operator when you set up your free Viz-a-Phone account.

How Can You Get Started?

1. You must have a computer that has a modem or is connected to DSL service.
2. Download the free Viz-a-Phone software available at this URL: *http://viz-a-phone.org/download*. Follow the easy, step-by-step instructions on our Web site.
3. Create a free Viz-a-Phone account.
4. Use any phone to dial the Viz-a-Phone service at 123-456-7890. Follow the on-screen instructions to **activate** your account. Now, you're ready to make your first call!

Benefits:

- You will have auditory support from your phone and visual support from your computer.
- You can control the size, color, and font style of the captions on the computer screen. This is very helpful if you have poor vision and need a large font.
- You can save and print the conversation captions from your computer.

The captioning service is funded by the Telecommunications Relay Service as part of Title IV of the Americans with Disabilities Act (ADA).

*Note: The specific product shown in this advertisement is fictional; however, there are similar products available. You can search for these online.

Public Service Advertisement

VIZ-A-PHONE

Directions: Darken the best answer choice.

1. Viz-a-Phone is meant to help people who cannot
   - Ⓐ hear clearly.
   - Ⓑ see clearly.
   - Ⓒ move their arms.
   - Ⓓ speak.

2. The word **activate** means to
   - Ⓐ request.
   - Ⓑ start up.
   - Ⓒ cancel.
   - Ⓓ improve.

3. Of these events, which one happens third?
   - Ⓐ A deaf woman uses Viz-a-Phone to call her daughter's school.
   - Ⓑ A deaf woman reads this public service announcement.
   - Ⓒ A deaf woman opens a free Viz-a-Phone account.
   - Ⓓ A deaf woman downloads Viz-a-Phone software onto her computer.

4. What is the most expensive part of the Viz-a-Phone service?
   - Ⓐ buying the Viz-a-Phone software
   - Ⓑ starting a Viz-a-Phone account
   - Ⓒ making a Viz-a-Phone call with an operator
   - Ⓓ It doesn't cost anything to use Viz-a-Phone.

5. Viz-a-Phone captioning is most similar to
   - Ⓐ text messaging.
   - Ⓑ subtitles on a DVD movie.
   - Ⓒ e-mail messages.
   - Ⓓ surfing the Web.

. Why is this service called Viz-a-Phone?
   - Ⓐ It makes the words in a phone call visible on a computer screen.
   - Ⓑ It was created by someone whose last name was Vizaphone.
   - Ⓒ It amplifies the words in a phone call so that the person can hear them better.
   - Ⓓ It translates international calls from a foreign language into English.

Native American Unsolved Mysteries

Of all the world's unsolved mysteries, those about Native Americans may be the most interesting. Great civilizations rose. Then, they vanished without leaving any sign of what caused their downfall. The people made amazing artwork. They built magnificent architecture. We wonder how and why. But because the people left no written language, our questions may never be answered.

This book is thoroughly researched and beautifully photographed. It offers the most in-depth, up-to-date coverage of these mysteries, including:

The Lines on the Nazcan Plateau

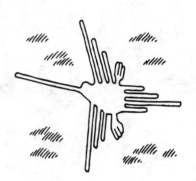

Between the towns of Nazca and Palpa in Peru are a series of spectacular **geoglyphs**. They stretch for fifty miles across the plateau. These huge pictures and thousands of perfectly straight lines have been preserved for about fourteen centuries. How? It is a dry, almost windless climate. These drawings are so clear and accurate that they must have been made by humans. We can only see them from the sky by looking down from helicopters and airplanes. The Native Americans who created them could not even see the finished pictures! So why—and how—did they make them?

Great Serpent Mound

Scattered across the American Midwest are mounds of varying sizes and shapes. The people who made them did not have the wheel. They built these mounds carrying baskets of dirt by hand. From the size and complexity of these earth mounds, it's clear that some would have taken hundreds of years to make. One is the Great Serpent Mound in Ohio. It is a snake over 1,300 feet long. Ten bears and a bird are found within a forest in Iowa. The shapes are only clear from an overhead view. Both the purpose of these mound and the disappearance of this great culture are shrouded in mystery.

The Anasazi?

More than 800 years ago, the Anasazi lived in the Four Corners are of the American Southwest. The land was dry. Yet they grew crops through the use of ditches. They carved their homes into the cliffs. Some of these homes still exist. We call these people the Anasazi But archaeologists know that was not their real name. Their name just one part of the mystery that occurred when they vanished. Th was about 700 years ago. No one knows what happened to them Their villages show no signs of war, hunger, or disease.

These and more mysteries are detailed within. Read and be mystified!

Native American Unsolved Mysteries

Of all the world's unsolved mysteries, those surrounding the Native Americans may be the most fascinating. Great civilizations rose and then disappeared without leaving any sign of what caused their downfall. The people made amazing artwork. They built magnificent architecture. We wonder how and why. But because the people left no written language, our questions may never be answered.

This book, thoroughly researched and beautifully photographed, offers the most in-depth, up-to-date coverage of these mysteries, including:

The Lines on the Nazcan Plateau

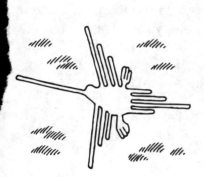

Between the towns of Nazca and Palpa in Peru lie a series of spectacular **geoglyphs** that stretch for fifty miles across the plateau. These gigantic pictures plus thousands of perfectly straight lines have been preserved for fourteen centuries in the dry, almost windless climate. These drawings are so clear and accurate that they must have been created by humans. We can only see them by looking down from helicopters and airplanes. This means that the Native Americans who created them could not even see the finished pictures! So why—and how—did they create them?

Great Serpent Mound

Scattered across the American Midwest are mounds of varying sizes and shapes. Since the people who made them did not have the wheel, they must have built these earthworks by carrying baskets of dirt by hand. From the size and complexity of the mounds, it appears that some would have taken centuries to make. The Great Serpent Mound in Ohio is a snake over 1,300 feet long. Ten bears and a bird are found within a forest in Iowa. The shapes are only clear from an overhead view. Both the purpose of these mounds and the disappearance of this great culture are shrouded in mystery.

The Anasazi?

More than 800 years ago, the Anasazi lived in the Four Corners area of the American Southwest. The land was dry, so they used irrigation to farm. They carved their homes into the cliffs. Some were so well made that they still exist. Although we call them the Anasazi, archaeologists know that that was not their actual name. Their name is part of their mystery. They disappeared about 700 years ago. No one knows what became of them. Their villages show no signs of war, famine, or disease.

These and more mysteries are detailed within. Read and be mystified!

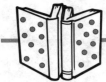

Native American Unsolved Mysteries

Of all the world's unsolved mysteries, the ones concerning Native Americans may be the most intriguing. Great civilizations rose and then vanished without any indication of what caused their downfall. They created amazing artwork and sophisticated architecture that has left us wondering how and why. Because the people had no written language, these questions may never be answered.

This book, thoroughly researched and beautifully photographed, offers the most in-depth, up-to-date coverage of these mysteries, including:

The Lines on the Nazcan Plateau

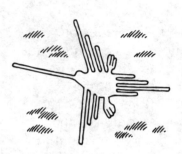

Stretching across fifty miles of the plateau between the towns of Nazca and Palpa in Peru are a series of spectacular **geoglyphs**. These enormous pictures and thousands of perfectly straight lines have been preserved for at least fourteen centuries by the dry, relatively windless climate. These drawings are so clear and accurate that they were definitely made by human hands. We can only see them from the vantage point of helicopters and airplanes. The Native Americans who created them could not! So why—and how—did they do it?

Great Serpent Mound

Scattered throughout the American Midwest are impressive mounds of varying sizes and shapes. Since the people who made them did not have the wheel, they must have built these earthworks by carrying baskets of dirt by hand. From the size and complexity of the mounds, it's clear that some would have taken centuries to build. In Ohio lies the Great Serpent Mound, a snake that is more than 1,300 feet long. Within a forest in Iowa are mounds in the shape of ten bears and a bird. The shapes are only clear from an overhead view. The purpose of these mounds and the disappearance of this great culture are shrouded in mystery.

The Anasazi?

More than 800 years ago, the Anasazi inhabited the Four Corners region of the American Southwest. Although the land was dry, they grew crops by using irrigation. They carved homes into the cliffs that were so well made that many of them still exist. We call them the Anasazi, yet archaeologists know that that was not their actual name. Their name is part of a mystery that began when they disappeared about 700 years ago. No one knows what became of them, and the villages show no signs of war, famine, or disease.

These and many more mysteries are detailed within. Read and be mystified!

Native American Unsolved Mysteries

Directions: Darken the best answer choice.

1. Great Serpent Mound is located
   Ⓐ near the Four Corners area of the American Southwest.
   Ⓑ in Nazca.
   Ⓒ in Palpa.
   Ⓓ in Ohio.

2. A **geoglyph** is a(n)
   Ⓐ earth mound in the shape of a snake, bear, or bird.
   Ⓑ ancient Native American alphabet.
   Ⓒ drawing on a cave wall.
   Ⓓ drawing on the ground.

3. In the creation of *Native American Unsolved Mysteries*, which event happened last?
   Ⓐ The author did research about Native Americans.
   Ⓑ The author wrote the manuscript.
   Ⓒ The book jacket was printed.
   Ⓓ The book was edited.

4. Why might we *never* find the answers to these mysteries?
   Ⓐ There is no evidence left of Native American culture before the 1700s.
   Ⓑ Without written records, we can only guess at what happened.
   Ⓒ Today's Native Americans believe they must keep these secrets sacred.
   Ⓓ The government of Peru will not allow anyone to study the geoglyphs.

5. We know that the Native Americans who built their homes into the cliffs near the Four Corners area had a tribal name. It is
   Ⓐ not definitely known.
   Ⓑ Anasazi.
   Ⓒ Nazca.
   Ⓓ Palpa.

People made the Nazcan Plateau lines around the year
   Ⓐ 600 CE.
   Ⓑ 800 CE.
   Ⓒ 1200 CE.
   Ⓓ 1400 CE.

Answer Sheet

Name: _____

Title: _____

Page: _____

1. Ⓐ   Ⓑ   Ⓒ   Ⓓ
2. Ⓐ   Ⓑ   Ⓒ   Ⓓ
3. Ⓐ   Ⓑ   Ⓒ   Ⓓ
4. Ⓐ   Ⓑ   Ⓒ   Ⓓ
5. Ⓐ   Ⓑ   Ⓒ   Ⓓ
6. Ⓐ   Ⓑ   Ⓒ   Ⓓ

Answer Sheet

Name: _____

Title: _____

Page: _____

1. Ⓐ   Ⓑ   Ⓒ   Ⓓ
2. Ⓐ   Ⓑ   Ⓒ   Ⓓ
3. Ⓐ   Ⓑ   Ⓒ   Ⓓ
4. Ⓐ   Ⓑ   Ⓒ   Ⓓ
5. Ⓐ   Ⓑ   Ⓒ   Ⓓ
6. Ⓐ   Ⓑ   Ⓒ   Ⓓ

Answer Sheet

Name: _____

Title: _____

Page: _____

1. Ⓐ   Ⓑ   Ⓒ   Ⓓ
2. Ⓐ   Ⓑ   Ⓒ   Ⓓ
3. Ⓐ   Ⓑ   Ⓒ   Ⓓ
4. Ⓐ   Ⓑ   Ⓒ   Ⓓ
5. Ⓐ   Ⓑ   Ⓒ   Ⓓ
6. Ⓐ   Ⓑ   Ⓒ   Ⓓ

Answer Sheet

Name: _____

Title: _____

Page: _____

1. Ⓐ   Ⓑ   Ⓒ   Ⓓ
2. Ⓐ   Ⓑ   Ⓒ   Ⓓ
3. Ⓐ   Ⓑ   Ⓒ   Ⓓ
4. Ⓐ   Ⓑ   Ⓒ   Ⓓ
5. Ⓐ   Ⓑ   Ⓒ   Ⓓ
6. Ⓐ   Ⓑ   Ⓒ   Ⓓ

Answer Sheet

Name: _____

page 17
1. Ⓐ Ⓑ Ⓒ Ⓓ
2. Ⓐ Ⓑ Ⓒ Ⓓ
3. Ⓐ Ⓑ Ⓒ Ⓓ
4. Ⓐ Ⓑ Ⓒ Ⓓ
5. Ⓐ Ⓑ Ⓒ Ⓓ
6. Ⓐ Ⓑ Ⓒ Ⓓ

page 37
1. Ⓐ Ⓑ Ⓒ Ⓓ
2. Ⓐ Ⓑ Ⓒ Ⓓ
3. Ⓐ Ⓑ Ⓒ Ⓓ
4. Ⓐ Ⓑ Ⓒ Ⓓ
5. Ⓐ Ⓑ Ⓒ Ⓓ
6. Ⓐ Ⓑ Ⓒ Ⓓ

page 57
1. Ⓐ Ⓑ Ⓒ Ⓓ
2. Ⓐ Ⓑ Ⓒ Ⓓ
3. Ⓐ Ⓑ Ⓒ Ⓓ
4. Ⓐ Ⓑ Ⓒ Ⓓ
5. Ⓐ Ⓑ Ⓒ Ⓓ
6. Ⓐ Ⓑ Ⓒ Ⓓ

page 77
1. Ⓐ Ⓑ Ⓒ Ⓓ
2. Ⓐ Ⓑ Ⓒ Ⓓ
3. Ⓐ Ⓑ Ⓒ Ⓓ
4. Ⓐ Ⓑ Ⓒ Ⓓ
5. Ⓐ Ⓑ Ⓒ Ⓓ
6. Ⓐ Ⓑ Ⓒ Ⓓ

page 21
1. Ⓐ Ⓑ Ⓒ Ⓓ
2. Ⓐ Ⓑ Ⓒ Ⓓ
3. Ⓐ Ⓑ Ⓒ Ⓓ
4. Ⓐ Ⓑ Ⓒ Ⓓ
5. Ⓐ Ⓑ Ⓒ Ⓓ
6. Ⓐ Ⓑ Ⓒ Ⓓ

page 41
1. Ⓐ Ⓑ Ⓒ Ⓓ
2. Ⓐ Ⓑ Ⓒ Ⓓ
3. Ⓐ Ⓑ Ⓒ Ⓓ
4. Ⓐ Ⓑ Ⓒ Ⓓ
5. Ⓐ Ⓑ Ⓒ Ⓓ
6. Ⓐ Ⓑ Ⓒ Ⓓ

page 61
1. Ⓐ Ⓑ Ⓒ Ⓓ
2. Ⓐ Ⓑ Ⓒ Ⓓ
3. Ⓐ Ⓑ Ⓒ Ⓓ
4. Ⓐ Ⓑ Ⓒ Ⓓ
5. Ⓐ Ⓑ Ⓒ Ⓓ
6. Ⓐ Ⓑ Ⓒ Ⓓ

page 81
1. Ⓐ Ⓑ Ⓒ Ⓓ
2. Ⓐ Ⓑ Ⓒ Ⓓ
3. Ⓐ Ⓑ Ⓒ Ⓓ
4. Ⓐ Ⓑ Ⓒ Ⓓ
5. Ⓐ Ⓑ Ⓒ Ⓓ
6. Ⓐ Ⓑ Ⓒ Ⓓ

page 25
1. Ⓐ Ⓑ Ⓒ Ⓓ
2. Ⓐ Ⓑ Ⓒ Ⓓ
3. Ⓐ Ⓑ Ⓒ Ⓓ
4. Ⓐ Ⓑ Ⓒ Ⓓ
5. Ⓐ Ⓑ Ⓒ Ⓓ
6. Ⓐ Ⓑ Ⓒ Ⓓ

page 45
1. Ⓐ Ⓑ Ⓒ Ⓓ
2. Ⓐ Ⓑ Ⓒ Ⓓ
3. Ⓐ Ⓑ Ⓒ Ⓓ
4. Ⓐ Ⓑ Ⓒ Ⓓ
5. Ⓐ Ⓑ Ⓒ Ⓓ
6. Ⓐ Ⓑ Ⓒ Ⓓ

page 65
1. Ⓐ Ⓑ Ⓒ Ⓓ
2. Ⓐ Ⓑ Ⓒ Ⓓ
3. Ⓐ Ⓑ Ⓒ Ⓓ
4. Ⓐ Ⓑ Ⓒ Ⓓ
5. Ⓐ Ⓑ Ⓒ Ⓓ
6. Ⓐ Ⓑ Ⓒ Ⓓ

page 85
1. Ⓐ Ⓑ Ⓒ Ⓓ
2. Ⓐ Ⓑ Ⓒ Ⓓ
3. Ⓐ Ⓑ Ⓒ Ⓓ
4. Ⓐ Ⓑ Ⓒ Ⓓ
5. Ⓐ Ⓑ Ⓒ Ⓓ
6. Ⓐ Ⓑ Ⓒ Ⓓ

page 29
1. Ⓐ Ⓑ Ⓒ Ⓓ
2. Ⓐ Ⓑ Ⓒ Ⓓ
3. Ⓐ Ⓑ Ⓒ Ⓓ
4. Ⓐ Ⓑ Ⓒ Ⓓ
5. Ⓐ Ⓑ Ⓒ Ⓓ
6. Ⓐ Ⓑ Ⓒ Ⓓ

page 49
1. Ⓐ Ⓑ Ⓒ Ⓓ
2. Ⓐ Ⓑ Ⓒ Ⓓ
3. Ⓐ Ⓑ Ⓒ Ⓓ
4. Ⓐ Ⓑ Ⓒ Ⓓ
5. Ⓐ Ⓑ Ⓒ Ⓓ
6. Ⓐ Ⓑ Ⓒ Ⓓ

page 69
1. Ⓐ Ⓑ Ⓒ Ⓓ
2. Ⓐ Ⓑ Ⓒ Ⓓ
3. Ⓐ Ⓑ Ⓒ Ⓓ
4. Ⓐ Ⓑ Ⓒ Ⓓ
5. Ⓐ Ⓑ Ⓒ Ⓓ
6. Ⓐ Ⓑ Ⓒ Ⓓ

page 89
1. Ⓐ Ⓑ Ⓒ Ⓓ
2. Ⓐ Ⓑ Ⓒ Ⓓ
3. Ⓐ Ⓑ Ⓒ Ⓓ
4. Ⓐ Ⓑ Ⓒ Ⓓ
5. Ⓐ Ⓑ Ⓒ Ⓓ
6. Ⓐ Ⓑ Ⓒ Ⓓ

page 33
1. Ⓐ Ⓑ Ⓒ Ⓓ
2. Ⓐ Ⓑ Ⓒ Ⓓ
3. Ⓐ Ⓑ Ⓒ Ⓓ
4. Ⓐ Ⓑ Ⓒ Ⓓ
5. Ⓐ Ⓑ Ⓒ Ⓓ
6. Ⓐ Ⓑ Ⓒ Ⓓ

page 53
1. Ⓐ Ⓑ Ⓒ Ⓓ
2. Ⓐ Ⓑ Ⓒ Ⓓ
3. Ⓐ Ⓑ Ⓒ Ⓓ
4. Ⓐ Ⓑ Ⓒ Ⓓ
5. Ⓐ Ⓑ Ⓒ Ⓓ
6. Ⓐ Ⓑ Ⓒ Ⓓ

page 73
1. Ⓐ Ⓑ Ⓒ Ⓓ
2. Ⓐ Ⓑ Ⓒ Ⓓ
3. Ⓐ Ⓑ Ⓒ Ⓓ
4. Ⓐ Ⓑ Ⓒ Ⓓ
5. Ⓐ Ⓑ Ⓒ Ⓓ
6. Ⓐ Ⓑ Ⓒ Ⓓ

page 93
1. Ⓐ Ⓑ Ⓒ Ⓓ
2. Ⓐ Ⓑ Ⓒ Ⓓ
3. Ⓐ Ⓑ Ⓒ Ⓓ
4. Ⓐ Ⓑ Ⓒ Ⓓ
5. Ⓐ Ⓑ Ⓒ Ⓓ
6. Ⓐ Ⓑ Ⓒ Ⓓ

Answer Key

page 17
1. B
2. A
3. D
4. C
5. B
6. D

page 21
1. A
2. B
3. C
4. D
5. A
6. B

page 25
1. C
2. A
3. D
4. C
5. B
6. A

page 29
1. D
2. C
3. B
4. A
5. D
6. B

page 33
1. C
2. D
3. A
4. B
5. C
6. A

page 37
1. B
2. D
3. C
4. C
5. A
6. B

page 41
1. D
2. C
3. D
4. A
5. B
6. A

page 45
1. D
2. A
3. D
4. D
5. B
6. C

page 49
1. B
2. D
3. B
4. C
5. A
6. D

page 53
1. B
2. C
3. D
4. B
5. A
6. D

page 57
1. A
2. D
3. C
4. B
5. C
6. A

page 61
1. C
2. B
3. B
4. C
5. D
6. A

page 65
1. D
2. A
3. B
4. C
5. D
6. A

page 69
1. C
2. D
3. A
4. D
5. B
6. A

page 73
1. B
2. B
3. A
4. C
5. D
6. D

page 77
1. B
2. A
3. A
4. B
5. A
6. C

page 81
1. C
2. B
3. D
4. A
5. A
6. C

page 85
1. D
2. B
3. B
4. C
5. C
6. D

page 89
1. A
2. B
3. C
4. D
5. B
6. A

page 93
1. D
2. D
3. C
4. B
5. A
6. A